PRINCIP_
OF THE
UNIVERSE

PRINCIPLES
OF THE
UNIVERSE

Keith Casburn

First published in 1995 by
The College of Psychic Studies
16 Queensberry Place, London, SW7 2EB

British Library Cataloguing-in-Publication Data

A catalogue record of this book
is available from The British Library
ISBN 0 903336 28 6

Typeset, printed and bound in Great Britain by
Whitstable Litho, Whitstable, Kent.

CONTENTS

BIOGRAPHY

Keith Casburn was born and raised in Galway, Republic of Ireland. He spent two years studying general science at University College, Galway before training as an actor in the UK. He spent eleven years working in theatre and television as an actor and director before being drawn into Executive Search as a research consultant. Two years prolonged illness finally brought him into an understanding of himself, his psychic gifts and healing potential. He has been working full time as a psychic and healer since 1991.

ACKNOWLEDGEMENTS

To my parents who lovingly gave practical support through this period.

Christine McCarroll who patiently listened to the tapes and transcribed them.

Brenda Marshall and The College of Psychic Studies for allowing this to take place within its building.

Elizabeth Farrell who recognised the potential and guided me to where I am now.

Rupert Soskin for his imaginative interpretation of this text.

Jean Prince my editor for her creative and slavish input.

Dudley Poplak, President of The College of Psychic Studies, without whose support and encouragement I would not be bringing this document to print.

Lastly to Adrian King whose love and patience have meant more than I could voice.

FOREWORD

Spine erect, strong feeling of unease, a sense of mind being raised to a vibratory level that borders on being uncomfortable. There is a sense of familiarity about this contact, this energy, but the alertness creates a coarseness of being that is not entirely comfortable. A pause. Adjustments are made. I wait. Then something creates the impulse to speak.

The time is September 1992 and the place is the Lecture Hall at The College of Psychic Studies, London. There are twenty-six other people waiting to listen to what comes out of my mouth. My nervousness is extreme, which only adds to my general perplexed condition as to why I am leaving myself open in such a way when I have no preconceived idea of what will happen. But to put all of this in context I need to go back a little further.

In March 1991, while working with a group of colleagues at The College of Psychic Studies, a series of images led to a complete rise of my Kundalini. To describe any experience, which is deeply personal and only pertinent to the person involved, with any sense of objectivity is difficult. It would be impossible to relay what was involved – that is a book in itself – suffice to say that I was brought into contact with an absolute force of truth and wisdom that was compassionate and loving in a way I had never before experienced. This left me feeling very small, privileged, needed and worthy. Other indications were also given that I am unable to speak of. The aftershock lasted for several weeks and I was unable to work for three days. At that time, I was still working as a research consultant and although I was aware I would stop working in that field at some point, I was not at that time wholly sure as to when or how. But by the end of the following month, I had relinquished my job and in a complete act of trust, I started as a full time psychic and healer. Had I known what I was about to go through, who knows if I would have made the same decision as I did.

The rise of my Kundalini brought with it a rapport with a level of understanding that I could never have conceived of before that time. It was as though the whole Akashic records were stored in my head and I literally had access to all understanding. I asked what I had to do with this understanding and the response was "nothing". I was told that this knowledge would be drawn from me as required, that I was the keeper of the books in the library. I knew where the information was stored, and I only had to make it available when it was asked for or needed. This was both equally frustrating and satisfying and was my first object lesson in being, not doing.

Another interesting development had taken place as well. In my training as a medium and psychic, I had three specific guides who identified themselves as personalities who worked with different aspects of my being: Thoth, who is Egyptian, to extend my philosophical awareness; Walter, who is German, to make communication more practical; Dzhan, Chinese, a light sprite to bring me joy. They all now stepped away to be replaced by a consciousness that I can only describe as Master. No personality, name or attributes. Definitely not a guide, as he did not advise, but merely provoked questions. I was taught to understand the questions which meant that the answers were inherently understood. The more I understood, the less I was aware of

Master presence. Any insecurity on my part was dealt with by seeming impatience. No time for that any more. Second lesson in objectivity – if I hadn't learnt to trust by now, tough!

Events then really started to become more lively. Between late 1991 and spring 1992 my material life fell apart. All structures, including my beliefs, literally fell away. I became nothing and experienced bliss. Bliss was something, surely, that we encountered when everything was going well. Wrong again. My life was falling apart, or so it seemed, yet here I was in this extraordinary state. What had actually happened unbeknownst to myself, was that I had become so battered and bruised I had let go of everything. Life now returned with a different message in a new context. Finally I had become responsible to me. With this fresh perspective, I started to rebuild my internal and external life. This was when my 'journeys' began.

Early one morning, in preparation for meditation, something happened that I can only describe as part of my mind left my being and journeyed into space. Three days later it 'arrived' at some other physical point in the universe. It created a synthesis between me and a consciousness that I had never experienced before. An energy form literally came into my being and became 'half of me'. A gold body with a detached sense, part of me and yet not part of me. It seemed to create a bridge across time and space that allowed an energy flow between me and somewhere else. It is difficult for me to illustrate or tell what happened over the resulting period as it was and still is deeply personal. But I was introduced to other beings who greeted me as one of them – I mean this within the meditative not the physical sense. By other beings I don't mean what we have come to understand as spiritual beings, or those who are part of the spiritual reality. They were cosmic beings, forms of intelligence or consciousness which exist now in other dimensions of physical space. I came to know their needs which, fundamentally, are to communicate with us, to themselves, to other forms within the universe, so that there is continuity of information that can maintain balance.

The Aboriginal people have song lines that allow them to cross vast tracts of barren land and by using these song lines they can always know where they are at any given moment. In the same way, there are similar routes through Space that allow those who know how to use them to make contact with other forms of intelligence or consciousness, and to perpetuate or direct the flow of information through all time and space. These are only just being made known, but as I understand it, within the next fifteen to twenty years, there will be many other people who will be familiar with what I am saying now. To shorten a very long journey, my awareness during these communications seems to be suspended somewhere in free space, so that certain forms who wish to have a voice through my communication mechanism may do so. This is done not necessarily to guide, but to provoke awareness and understanding; to wake people up and make them more intelligent. It also means that this suspension can allow more than one source to enter into a discourse. So even though the illustrative source of consciousness may be consistently different, there is a certain unity about what is being said and why.

Coming back to that first evening in March 1991, this rather unusual communication was the start of my journey into a phase of understanding that now takes me into the context of cosmology. Through this I have been given how to relate emotionally, mentally and spiritually to the stars and planets in the heavens; the effect they have on our well-being and how we can draw on their energy being, not only for greater insight, but also to help us to resolve difficult and often repetitive actions in life.

As you read the text in this book, you will notice that the language becomes easier with each ensuing chapter. This relates to an erosion of my own resistance and also a certain stability which my nervous system acquired as it became more familiar with the energy that streamed into my body. The text is literally as it was given. I have no emotional connection with it, as it didn't pass through my conceptual mind.

This only leaves me now to thank those who were present, who contributed to drawing this information into the open, and to you, the reader, who may now wish to know more.

ONE

Consciousness Beyond Matter

Within the reality of silence there is all. For a moment close your eyes and visualise within your mind's eye the author, or, if you do not know him, just visualise his name. Focus your attention on that image and allow your mental energy to connect with it, projecting your mental energy-force towards it and allow a unity to be established, so that what was communicated, and is now written, can be absorbed at every level, both conscious and unconscious.

As this energy is projected back from the author's image or name, allow your mind to sense the energy emanating from this point, to sense a subtle change in bearing.

If you are still reading, stop for a moment and make this connection. When you open your eyes the circle of energy between you will be complete and the connection will be made.

Establish if you can a growing reality expanding within the mind.

We are righteous consciousness. We validate truth, we communicate concepts of reality beyond the concept of matter, to bring about objectivity of vision and comprehension, enabling a study to be made of the complementary nature of how aspects of consciousness interface with each other within the parameters of the universe.

We speak from beyond matter. We have no emotional context. We look, we observe, we see. We recognise things as they are. We have no influence of your emotional state, it is not part of our vibrational being. In your terms, we work at the level of higher mind, assimilating through knowledge which is provoked through understanding. This understanding pervades the entire universe within which everything is connected and interlinked in a variegated form of inter-relating communication. We stand at a focal point within this reality, and we seek to communicate truth as it is, rather than as it is interpreted.

We act as ambassadors for other consciousness forms within the physicality of the universe, that they may be transmitted to you in a form which is agreeable and acceptable. We work in co-operation with your spiritual reality, to enable you to understand propositions of energy-formations of structures of thought as they are enabling you to reach outside the parameters of your own mind, to grasp that which is elusive and often not justifiable within the parameters of your own existence.

You are but one body of evolving consciousness, moving towards recognition of soul self, as it is understood within your reality, so that this may become a vibrant force of who you are, so that the masks of deception are removed and displaced, thereby allowing truth to communicate its righteous self in all honesty and clarity, and be recognised and seen for what it is.

This is part of your evolution. This is part of the progression through which your society is propelling itself at this time towards a greater understanding of its needs. The veils of deception are slowly being removed enabling those who can to see the reality of the unfoldment, to see the cracks in the mask, and recognise the untruths.

All solid structures within your society are beginning to disintegrate, be these political or religious, in your terms, within the contained sense of the word 'belief'. You can no longer perpetuate your existence and growing enlightenment within these structures. That time is finished. It is gone. It has passed. You witnessed the passing of this period in time within the framework of 1992.

As a result, you are experiencing increasing turbulence. Objectively the turbulence has not increased, it is merely that which causes this which is more visible. There is nowhere for it to hide, consequently you perceive it within your sensory perceptions more, as all of these upheavals have vibratory states of being of their own. They echo throughout your land of Earth, they are felt within your emotional bodies and you rationalise their happenings with your conscious minds.

We are part of a sun-consciousness beyond your galaxy. We do not exist in the same time frame as your solar system. We are not a mirror image, but it would not be inaccurate to observe that we are a part of your reflection within the universe. Our purpose is to connect with those within your environment who can bring down the new, spiritual, master-energy that envelops your Earth into your reality, so that it may be communicated, so that those within your reality may sense, feel – within your understanding of the term feel – and recognise what this is, and then come to know the effect it will have.

As we speak, we are a composite compilation of both light and sound. Each composition has a different texture, tone and vibration within the minuteness of each particle of this

3

composition. There is a unique universe which can communicate to like-minded forms within its own reality of existence. To create communication of this nature entails a coming together of many different essences, textures of colours, vibrancy of tones, to envelop the projected mind of your speaker, to influence the tonality and vibrancy of that mind, to enable active communication to be effected. There has been much preparation to allow this now to come to fruition.

The emotional state of your speaker has been diminished to a point whereby it has little or no effect on how his mind communicates information. The speaker in question being in a more comfortable position while communicating, than being within his own physical, emotional body which would cause stress and displacement of the mind. Within the mind it is as though there are channels through which our energy can be conducted. These channels are shared in co-operation with other forms of consciousness, of intelligence, and will also communicate themselves to you. The realities you will be exposed to will be multiple, to allow you to embrace with a more total view the nature of who you are, who we are, and how we relate within the physical framework of the universe. Because of the density of your emotional body, it is not always possible for us to communicate directly orally with you, and for you to be able to facilitate understanding within our objectivity. In your terms there is a considerable language gap. Understand it. Understand that there may be some inconsistency with how this information may be transmitted.

Your speaker is projecting his mind beyond the emotional spiritual reality to enable this discourse to take place but as this is taking place, because of the stress this places on his emotional body, there are some energies that cannot be revealed or transmitted. Also understand that you are hearing at more than one level. At the moment there is a part of your mind that is connected with this stream of energy that we call consciousness, allowing you to absorb the mental vibration of our very being. Over a period of time this process invokes in you an intelligence that enables the concepts that are projected in your way to be absorbed and understood within your own period of evolution as you may allow this to happen. Understand we only come together in this form to communicate. The composition of this current form is new. Once this form returns to its multiple state, it can be anywhere within the universe that has practical relevance to our being.

We work in co-operation with other forms. We monitor the evolution of your mind. In our terms we help to work with the adjustment of tonality of your mental vibration to enable you to hold, in descriptive terms, your future within the mind concept. We are aware of the parallel of where your Earth reality is in future time and where it exists now. We, therefore, attune the mind, as it is now in your presence, to adjust it to the coming future so that the attractability, and the magnetism that is created between both realities in time, have a consistency and a progression making sure that at each step of the way you do not experience anything beyond your tolerance.

We cannot approach many. We guide, if you like, others to do this on our behalf as we are part of the sound vibration within the universe, consequently there are tunnels through which we can pass quite freely throughout the whole of the universe without friction or impediment. Our sound is heard throughout all. This is not confined by time or space, but sets up a resonance within which we have total freedom of movement through each dimension, through each galaxy, through each system of intelligence or consciousness as it is

5

understood by you.

We are not a fixed reality. There is no world in your terms to which we are attracted, or on which we reside. There is a magnetic point within our galaxy where we regroup, where we come to communicate, where we attract the higher minds of those who can make the journey to us. This magnetic point is mathematically programmable. It is a constant. It is a fixed point, though there is no fixed physical reality. We not only attune the mind of your own earth vibrations, but we also facilitate connections throughout the universe of other consciousness forms who seek to communicate by this vibrational telepathy, so that there is a consistency in the flow of communication throughout, so that changes within the whole can be observed and worked with without having to adjust our own spatial arrangement.

We tend to work with a slightly denser form of communication within the physical framework of the universe; to concentrate on linking each with each so there is a consistency of awareness of what is happening. This is then passed on to another realm so that it, in turn, may observe the spontaneous evolution that it too, as ambassador to its own realm, may therefore pass on to the next.

All your belief structures are being taken away. All of that upon which you have relied is redundant. The cosmic stickiness that has allowed these beliefs to be perpetuated no longer exists. Dependence has gone. Responsibilities and self-reliance are becoming more vibrant. There is nothing else left except who each of you are, in reality to yourselves and to your own connection with the God-source, realising that your connection with your source is all that is, and within this you have what you need.

By allowing this to become conscious and active in your mind you are hurrying towards your own natural states of divinity – thereby releasing yourselves from dense contracts within your earthly environment, allowing you to embrace higher laws, and thereby giving you an opportunity to experience the consistency of the philosophy of all that is within the universe

The Transformative Leap

Understand the principles for all are the same. There is no deviation. Everything exists within consistent parameters. Consciousness from the God-source is. It is consistent. We belong to it. We respond to it and we evolve with it. There is no stillness. It is progressive. You are approaching a time when the dense laws to which you have been subject are now being withdrawn. Within the time framework of your own lives as they are on Earth, you are going to bring about this radical change, so that your need to experience the emotional reality to further growth, to further your haste towards your divine Self, will no longer be needed. The communication will come through the higher mind bringing about an expansion outside of your physical body. There will be a need for this to be brought down through the physical body for this understanding to be made practical.

You are not, in the near future, going to lose your emotions, your emotional bodies, but understand that as there are levels within the energetic field surrounding your body, these are reflected outwards into the universe, allowing you to experience their realities as they are within the outward expression. Consequently, for you to absorb the clarity of things, of matter, of anti-matter, as they are, it is necessary for these various levels within your energetic bodies to be clear, to be unconstricted.

In many ways your energy centres, the chakras within the

body, are but knots which will be untied. Once they have been released and cleared, it is as though they do not exist. So you become consciousness and you exist side by side with consciousness, without friction, in perpetual motion, still being able to experience the emotional reality but in its own truth. When this point arises you will be free from the emotional karma as it exists, which regulates the body of learning in itself. It will be made redundant. The stress on the physical will no longer be there, consequently the memory contained within the cellular body will offer itself in surrender to this heightened awareness bringing about total absorption to this energy field of existence. It is at this point that you will become pure consciousness.

As you stand through time, your place within your time-scale is nearing completion. There will be separation within your environment of those who can make this transform-ative leap, and those, through their own limitations of growth, who are incapable of recognising the possibility of these other realities, and who, in future time, will not be able to sustain themselves within the evolved physical reality as it will be. Consequently their consciousness, their very spiritual being, will remain within the astral spiritual state and will communicate, relate and work with those who be-come reincarnate once again from that level.

It is those spirit essences who have made the trans-formative leap, who have let the physical body respond to the mind-impulse, who have allowed their own cellular memory to adapt to this future transformation, as it is making itself known in the present, who will be able to take this memory into the spiritual state, and return it once again to the new physical body that it will require in future time. This means it is already emotionally prepared. The spirit will fit the body. The spirit will be able to adapt to the body. The body in itself will be able to contain that particular vibration. Those who cannot make this transition will not. Their time here in your environment will be terminated. This is not with any sense of judgement. It is with a sense of recognition of the reality as it is.

The DNA structure within your physical bodies is entering its final state of transformation. The energetic impulses between certain protein combinations are being altered, so that the activation of memory within the physical body is preparing it, and you, to be able to have some sort of precognitive sense of where it needs to be in future time. As you experience the taking away of dependency, the memory within your cellular structure will jettison certain impulses which are no longer required; in your terminology – creating space to absorb more. The process is much like that of the intake of breath within the lungs, so that as you expel the air you create a vacuum, thereby creating a latent energy to be able to draw inside yourselves part of the life force.

By jettisoning some of this memory you are creating, in your terminology, a 'black hole' which will attract within it whatever consciousness you decide to feed it. This is entirely relevant to your own development and evolution. It means that whatever you jettison within your own reality, whatever level your spiritual clarity is at, at that point in time, that is what you will draw in at a cellular level. You will not draw into that anything outside of your experience or your ability to tolerate. Everything will be within your spectrum of resonance.

You have a certain vibration and that in actuality permeates through time consistently, giving out a form of cosmic attraction which will draw to it whatever it needs, at any given point in time, but nothing outside that vibratory spectrum. This means that you cannot be interfered with.

What you do, what you achieve, is by your own merit and effort. Understand it is all of your own volition, choice and ability to accept. Many of you project your minds into other realities and are unable to accept what is presented, consequently, the possibility of raising your vibration up to that level does not occur. As a result, you do not attract to you that which you cannot accept. It is a consistent safety mechanism that works with all living intelligence within the physical framework of the universe.

The time has come for you to use, to actively put into motion, into practice, your own self-sufficiency. Each of you has the ability to create awareness for yourselves without help. That is the actuality. Because of the density of your being, there may be need to seek affirmation within that density of being, but you will come to know and trust that who you are, and what you know, is true and accurate. Your reality receives much information from many different quarters of the universe, often much of this conflicting. Understand that those who receive this information are at different stages of evolution. Because of the vagaries of evolution it is not always possible to accurately convey `that what is', nor, because of the density of the beings who receive this communication, is it possible for them to release their own minds sufficiently to allow accuracy to be conveyed.

What we are telling you is that there is much relevance within all. We merely say, be discerning. A lot of what is conveyed is contained within metaphors as often this is the only way in which certain aspects can be communicated, namely within a certain disguise, as the reality in its truthful sense makes it blunt and challenging in a way that you might not accept. Within the reality of the situation in which you are sitting there are also some concepts over this fixed period which may be difficult to absorb.

A Time of Change

You may be wondering when, in your time reality, such changes, such evolution will occur. Let us say that it is happening now. With no sense of disrespect, you go around the world with your eyes closed. You perceive only the density of your own reality. You do not see those who are actually not what they seem. There are cosmic beings who have exchanged bodies, with permission, with those who are part of the emotional-spiritual evolution, to gain first-hand observation within the dense body, enabling these cosmic beings to transmit to other parts of the universe how constructively assistance may be given. There are those elements outside your conscious visible spectrum that do not allow you to see those cosmic beings who are on Earth, who work in tandem with those physical beings who can be alert to what needs transmitting.

We talk of those who exist, certain mathematical scholars, who work with spiritual teachers and with people who themselves work with the Earth itself. Many of you work in resonance with certain cosmic beings, who monitor and assist your vibrational change as you reach out to seek consciousness, helping you to adapt. Remember that you are cosmic, we are cosmic, we work in co-operation, we look after your physical well-being. This is usually translated by your spiritual reality which has experience of your emotional sensibilities.

You are part of an exciting movement in time when the superficiality of your society as it exists is being removed. Those of you who can respond and adapt will become strong and by example show what is possible. The vibrational nature of your very being is changing by the second. Words cannot accurately convey the process, the movement and the adaptability that you display towards this evocative impulse that is working with you at this time, which you understand as the Christ consciousness. There is a need for all of you at some point to be Christed, to accept your rightful divinity, that you may enjoy your rightful place within the spiritual realms as part of a cohesive whole of the loving Godhead. It is towards this that you work. It is with this that we relate. And it is with this, largely, that all or most of the cosmic impulse is translated through. You are experiencing cellular change, memory change, protein change. You experience it in a subtle way so that there is no imbalance in the physical body in a way that you are not able to respond to. You experience it, and you recognise it as emotional pain. It has started, you are part of it.

If we look at the possibility of speed, then this is increasing the rapidity with which the Earth is experiencing its own evolution, which is why we say you must adapt, or you must leave.

You may ask, how do I adapt? Let us answer: you show by example, by who you are, by how you respond. Understand that you have an energetic field surrounding you. Every individual who comes into contact with that energetic field will experience in a microsecond what that reality means. It is part of how communication works. It is part of this raising of consciousness that you are experiencing. It is not necessarily the words of the teaching, it is the coming together of the energy as we come together to communicate to you. As you brush against someone else, energetically that is conveyed. They experience it. Understand that you only have to register something for the smallest fraction of time in order to understand it. The limitations that your own emotions place on you mean that you tend to need a continuing experience of various different realities. In actuality, it happens in the instant. What you get from the perpetuation is the comfort. It is this dependency that is being taken away, to show you that time is not required. What you will come to know is the speed in which you can now experience.

As you adapt, your cellular structure will change. You are organic, you are an organic being, you are composed largely of the elements of carbon, hydrogen and oxygen. You have a need for certain organic compounds in various different combinations. As your cellular structure changes, your organs will become smaller, your need or dependence on certain of the combinations of organic substances in and around your Earth will be required less. You panic as certain food substances are being used up within the Earth. Your planet is alerting you to the fact that there are limitations in what it can provide. Your memory as a conscious being on the Earth will respond naturally to that.

In general terms of time it means that a generation will be skipped before that information or transformation will be passed on in actuality. There are those among you whose skin composition is changing, who can no longer tolerate the energy from the sun in the way that you have been. Eventually this will gather momentum, it will drive people indoors, underground, under the ocean. It means you will draw more on the hidden resources, which are not utilised on a day-to-day basis at this present moment. Consequently, you will be able to manufacture for yourselves a different environment in which to live. You are adapting to your environment. As many doors are being closed to you, such as the failing atmosphere, the difficulties in providing means for heat and for power, then understand that soon what you take from the Earth will be given back to the Earth. We will talk later of radical changes that will occur within the Earth as a result of what is taken from it. Understand that there is adaptability here as you work in co-operation with those who assist.

The atmosphere around the Earth will become more ionised as the ozone layer erodes in certain places. The atmospheric climate of the Earth therefore will change. The habitual nature in which you express your leisure time will also change as you will no longer be able to tolerate open spaces in the way that you have previously. This is not only to do with the quality of the air, it is to do with certain destructions, physical destructions of the surface of your own Earth planet. You can, you will, and you are responding. In many ways it is too late to change quite a lot of what is happening, consequently there is a need to totally re-evaluate and redefine your habitual living space.

As we are sun-consciousness, we pay homage to you who have come to listen, who allow your minds to be elevated to levels of understanding beyond your emotional reality. Accept this energy, allow it to be drawn into your physical selves so that it may register within you. Allow that silent communication, that invisible communion between us and you, take this with you and make it yours within your own evolutionary pattern of evolvement. We look on you with love. We offer respect and we endeavour to serve to the best of our ability.

TWO

The Reality of Planet Earth

We would like now to introduce you to the first of several energy-structures that will be given throughout this book. Visualising these energy-structures will help your multi-dimensional mind to move with greater freedom, to access consciousness at other levels.

Visualise if you will, a square without substance, merely the lines of force delineating the shape of the square itself. Visualise a triangle bisecting the square, perpendicularly, merely concentrating on the lines of force, as there is no substance to the triangle.

Visualise another triangle, intersecting the square at right angles to the other triangle, so that you have the square encompassed within two triangles. All three structures are without substance, merely shape. Allow a beam of gold to descend, hitting the apex of both triangles as they are at one point, allowing all this structure to be infused with the colour gold. Mentally, place your mind within the structure, where you feel it is most comfortable.

Understanding that your mind is multi-dimensional and can be used as a projectile, leave an aspect of your mind within this space and draw the energy from this structure back towards yourself, so that it connects with your own mind as it connects with your physical reality. This structure, and others which will be presented to you, have a particular mathematical significance. They give your mind the opportunity to experience, at the mental level, a vibratory reality which you can absorb in your own time for your own progression and enlightenment. Know that this force which you ultimately are connected with – which has been downgraded sufficiently for each and every one of you to tolerate, and also for the subconscious part of yourself to absorb – may be elusive or lost by your conscious mind.

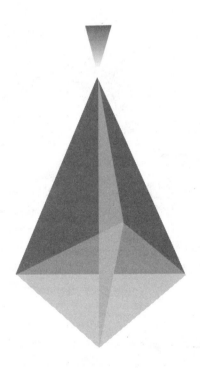

We have already spoken of who we are, of the coming together of a multi-faceted consciousness that is from a singular domain, of how the combination of these energies is new, bringing forth a vibrant form of communication which will instigate further contact within the Earth dimension. We wish to extend this now into our observation of your reality as we perceive it. Do understand that because of the nature of our reality, there are certain aspects of your experience in the Earth plane with which we have no comparable experience ourselves. As a result, often what might be said will seem cruel, or forcefully direct. It is our limitation of anticipating your emotional reaction to what is being conveyed. Always take from this what you feel is appropriate. Do not try to embrace that which is intolerable. Our communication is translated into words and, because of the frequency of some of the information, may be limited in its verbal expression.

We will endeavour to start from the inside out, working from the core of the Earth itself, expanding on the changes that are happening at an inter-terrestrial level, expanding it to the surface of your planet outwards into the cosmos, giving again our dispassionate view of how we observe evolution in your terms.

We must examine the Earth reality as it exists as we look on the Earth as a living organism. It is a very dense, contained force. It is compressed energy. It is compressed by the accumulation of many different substances within your galaxy, which has, through its own cosmic attractability, been brought together in a unifying force to provide a basis of consciousness. This enables cosmic intelligence and realities to experience consciousness within a very dense plane, enabling those other forces who co-operate to observe a progression, so that this may be used in future time to assist those who are also engaged in difficulty within the physical framework of the cosmos.

Within the core of the Earth, we have a red vibrant energy source, a molten mass in perpetual motion, creating continual friction, providing an energy source for its own living mechanism. The adjoining layers, as they extend outwards from the molten core, acquire greater density. It is cooler as friction is not present, allowing a denser dialogue to be maintained within the physical structure. The density of this mineral-being allows it to absorb high-frequency energies as they exist within the physical framework of the cosmos, allowing it to understand and recognise its own progression for itself, thereby enabling it to respond to whatever changes take place on its surface. Once you have passed the half-way mark towards the surface of the Earth, the density stops, giving way once more to friction, creating a greater variety of substance in various combinations to be able to maintain life-force on the surface of the Earth. These layers of less density are also in perpetual motion. They themselves continually adapt and redistribute themselves over the surface of the Earth beyond the half-way stage, knowing and understanding that any change there is, is from these layers outwards. They will enable each and every particular substance to respond to whatever stimulus has been placed within it. This is important to remember when we come to discuss, in later times, effects that have been created by your race on the surface of the Earth and how they are assimilated by the Earth itself.

Chaos and Rebirth

As we move further towards the surface of the Earth, we have carbon, hydrogen and oxygen in less density than is experienced towards the centre of the Earth. This means that there is greater fluidity and freedom of movement within many different vibrant layers of composition, each being complementary and interdependent upon the other. By saying this, it is understood that if any particular substance or mineral is removed completely from the Earth, chaos will result within that particular stratum beyond the half-way mark. In practical terms, it means the collapsing of land, the creating of greater substantial structures below the aqueous solutions that permeate the Earth itself, allowing this liquid motion to cover that which was once exposed. It allows the Earth, in simple terms, the opportunity to heal and regenerate itself, to be able once more to create those mineral structures that were once present, through friction and through the cosmic energy-consciousness that the Earth itself absorbs as a living mineral organism.

In your time, this requires thousands of years in passing. The ages with which you delineate the evolution of your Earth and its structure already demonstrate this, as there are periods when there is a predominance of a particular mineral proliferation that, ultimately, finds its own balance within time. These proliferations have been assisted in finding this balance with outside help, with assistance from beyond the Earth-being. We reach a time when the superficial surface of the Earth itself, the balance between land and water, has been created to sustain life within a density that is not normally experienced within the physical framework of the universe. By that, we do not say that you are unique in this experience, we merely say that this experience, in your terms, is rare. Understand also that the particular make-up of your Earth-being has necessitated bringing a spiritual reality through which you can reincarnate. It allows you to absorb the understanding you have attained in the Earth environment and to be able to absorb it in its totality in another energetic-being, before progressing again into an existence on the surface of Earth.

We reach the point where life, as you understand it, is sustainable. There are certain factors, certain nutritional combinations, that have been effective in awakening it to creative vibrancy to sustain your very being. We are talking at this stage compositionally of carbon, hydrogen and oxygen. You are of the Earth. The Earth is of you. The Earth in its very origin is carbon, hydrogen, oxygen. There are other minerals from elsewhere within the cosmos which are also deposited on and within your Earth. By the very nature of their crystalline structure, they are imbued with an energy from other realities. This does not mean that they are alive, in your terminology, nor however does it mean that they are dead, in your terms. We are merely indicating that they have a life potential of their own.

Therefore, as the Earth itself has compositionally taken on these structures within itself, you yourselves have also taken on board many of these mineral compositions within your own physical being. The effect of the placing of these minerals within your being is in direct proportion to those which are lodged within the Earth. The purpose of these placements is also complementary, enabling you to connect with those other physical intelligent forces within the framework of the universe, understanding that your body has the capability to adapt and change as it evolves through time, not only towards a spiritual realisation but also to a point where cosmic realisation becomes fact. Once this level has been achieved, you then become released as an intelligent force of your own initiative into universal realms of consciousness. Understanding the fundamental structure of your being dictates and proves that you are cosmic.

We return to the Earth. Within the mineral compo. the Earth's structures there is potential life-force. With energy there is a cosmic magnetism, a stickiness attractability which will draw towards it anything that it needs to sustain life. This word is used as an illustration as you do not recognise life within mineral form. This magnetism resonates in waves, virtually within tubes that intercommunicate with other physical forms within the universe, with other planets, with other moons, which also have within them a mineral composition that is within the same vibratory spectrum.

The Earth is regarded as being free-standing within your solar system, because of the density and specific gravity of its being, and because of how this relates to the other stars, planets and moons within your solar system which is freely suspended. It is not. Because of the various mineral compositions contained within the physicality of the Earth, and because each of these minerals vibrates within a particular energy substratum within the framework of the universe and the cosmos, the Earth is held very securely within a web or an energetic network that is firmly in place. This would imply that every physical structure within the universe is also held in this energetic web that permeates everything through time. This would not be entirely accurate, but within the limitations of communication that are available at the moment, it may be safely assumed that this is the closest explanation that can be given.

We have total interdependency, therefore any ripple that is felt within your Earth reality is also resonated throughout the whole framework of the physical universe. This is why it is essential for co-operation to exist within the universe, and why there is a need to diminish fear, in your terms, of extraterrestrial beings and their need to take over and control. We do say there are those energetic forms who have not fulfilled their true consciousness and seek to work in friction against co-operation, who do seek, for their own reasons, to operate in a contrary motion. At this point in time we only wish to say that the effects of what they do is minimal, and in reality nothing is achieved to upset the balance.

If, therefore, the Earth is held very firmly within an energetic structure within the universe, you – as Earth beings – by having traces of mineral composition within your own physical body, are also connected to these energetic networks and are also held very firmly within consciousness, within practical realities as they exist. As you evolve through time you will understand where these tubes of energy enter the physicality of your body and can release the impediments that limit your communication within these streams of consciousness as they are. When that time comes the life-force, as we see it, of these materials within your physical body will ignite and become real. They will be able, therefore, to sustain the consciousness that your mind has access to, and will be able to maintain your mental being within the energetic structure that goes beyond physical delineation. This means, therefore, that there will be no need for physical structure within your energetic being. When that point is reached you will also no longer be limited with emotions, though your understanding of their relevance will still be contained within the memory-banks of your understanding. It is at that point also where you and your spiritual Self become one, releasing you into the cosmic realm itself, allowing you to perpetuate your energetic being for all times.

Illusion

Within your technological society, there is a conflict. Within your energetic being, there is a conflict. Within your energetic being, the conflict is between what you should be, and what you know you want. Within your technological society, there is that which is in progress, and that which is within the illusion of society. By that, we mean there are creations of elements, of physical structures – physical structures actually not required – but because of the power and political sensibility of your society, these have become currency in themselves. We merely wish to say that this currency is an illusion, and as you have reached a point when all structures within your society are being dissolved, then this in turn, this illusion, will radiate as what it is. The conflicts that your energetic being is being presented with, allow you the opportunity to become that which you know you should.

If you allow yourselves to trust yourselves sufficiently then that is all that is required, thereby enabling you to displace what, as an illusion, is reflected from the conflict of the technological aspect within society, which in itself is an illusion.

There is a term called market-force that is based on the monetarist structure, which is endorsed by political reality. We must look briefly at what the political reality is. It is a structure created by the mind to manipulate, control and use. But as this is created by the conscious mind, it can also be taken away by the conscious mind, as that which is freely created can be freely dissolved. The projection of the mind into a belief structure is, in itself, an illusion – it does not exist. What does exist is the energetic power that has gone into creating this belief structure. So the energy is prevalent. The energy is real. But the concept is imaginary. Using this as an analogy: you – within your political, market-driven society – are living within an illusion. As you allow yourselves to be what you feel you need to be, you can connect with technology as it needs to be, and use that to help sustain the quality of life as it really is, as it is entitled to be, within the framework of the Earth.

The problems you experience within your society result from the fact that the illusion can no longer perpetuate itself. Understand that there are limits to what the conscious mind can conceptualise. It is constrained as it operates from very dense matter. The truly creative mind takes on board more than your own conscious reality can and embraces the spirit and the cosmos as a universal whole. Allow that to speak with your dense being as one. That is the only reality that is, nothing else.

You may have many questions about these illusions. But the illusions that are society, religion, politics, social structures – these illusions have been built by those who wish to manipulate. They are subject to the whims and fashions of time as it exists at the moment. If you ask a question in relation to these illusions, there is no question because you are questioning something that does not exist, relating to something that does not exist; something that at this time is dissolving and no longer has a presence within your Earth. If you ask about who you are and how to bring this vibrancy into being, if you ask for help in living who you are, these questions will be answered. Understand that there are those who are concerned with trivia, who seek truth within superficiality. Truth is, consciousness is, God is, you 'is' – so explore you, ask about you. Ask to know your-selves, so you can be you, more, with courage, with clarity, allowing your own wisdom to speak, bringing you to the point where you understand the question so the answer is not required.

To help you in this respect, just know your mind. We say your mind is free. It is the space vehicle that can move freely through time, through density of matter, through place situations. Any process that can allow your mind to vibrate above the level of the illusion in which you live, can allow you the facility to see and experience what is. The process does not matter. How it is achieved is insignificant. Whether this is experienced through your astral plane, connected within your psycho-emotional spiritual cycle, or whether you go beyond this into the physical universe itself to experience intelligence, consciousness, as it is, does not matter. Take and use whatever means is at your disposal. Trust your inner sense of knowing to guide you.

Many of you have reached the point when you can reach inside yourselves to gather the stardust and to look within it, to see who you are. You can scatter this stardust in the air and see the vibrancy of its being, and as that disappears you will see the reflections through time in your mind, you will feel them in your heart and see them in the universe. Allow yourselves now the opportunity to experience, as it is within experience. You, within the density of your being, have your proof.

THREE

The Passage Into Earth Consciousness

Visualise if you will, a platinum ray, a platinum rod of infinitesimal thinness, lodged vertically in the centre of a circle, erect and free-standing. At the apex of this rod, visualise a red, bulbous light There is a density about this colour red to protect all those who enter into it. Project your mind, if you can, inside the red light.

Once inside, see, or sense, a silver glow surrounding the red, at a little distance. Allow yourself to accept this frequency as the platinum rod is activated and begins to ever-so-slightly hum. You are now connected and are prepared to receive at all possible levels that which you will read.

Understand that as each period of time we spend together proceeds, another element, another structure, is put into place. This allows you to magnetise towards yourself and evoke into consciousness, what you already have within you, thus allowing you the opportunity to experience the vibratory whole. You still carry within you the energy structure of the previous visualisation, so you are building a complex, energetic matrix around your mind, to allow yourself to continuously be alerted to what is, as opposed to what you think is. The vibration which is being directed to you can have unbearable frequential and vibrational effects on your physical-emotional being. But visualising the energy-structure is a way of downgrading the frequency to give it, or rather, make it, tolerable. It also offers you the opportunity to assimilate that which is not possible to communicate through words.

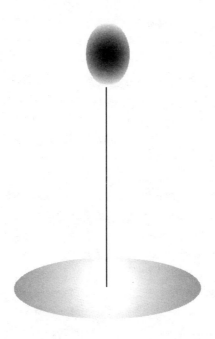

We have now spoken of the physical structure within the Earth, and how this is connected within the physical framework of the universe. We have reached the point where we wish to speak further about the dense physical and the energetic formation that you hold around you, which dictates what the physical is. The human being is a dense combination of psycho-emotional energy which has been brought together with a certain cosmic stickiness, or attraction, which is subject to a gravitational force, thereby keeping you connected to another consciousness form, which also has a dense physicality.

The human-being is subject to the physical-spiritual cycle, caught in perpetual motion until it reaches the divine state which it once left before it took on a dense physical form. This is how it is interpreted, and this is somewhat how it is viewed. This is not viewed in isolation, but for the moment we will talk about our observation of this cycle.

You are spirit. You are an energetic frequency that has experience of the psycho-emotional state. While being in a spiritual state, the vibrancy, the experience of that which you have endured on Earth is part of your energetic make-up, as in this state you are not subject to dense physical laws. You can view the universe in its entirety and observe your place and passageway through time with greater clarity, allowing you to see, know and understand what is further required in your evolutionary development through the psycho-emotional state.

Nothing you experience is lost. It is all remembered and put to practical use. As the realisation comes of the necessity for a physical incarnation, in your terms, you choose your time and you choose the circumstance that will facilitate your passage into physicality. This requires assistance within the spiritual realm to allow you to enter at the right angle, within the correct vibratory spectrum, giving you a clear passageway through which you can interpenetrate the Earth itself. As you are about to enter physical consciousness, you go through the process, again in your terms, of loss of memory of understanding, as you endure the density of being in the physical state. It is when you approach this lower vibratory consciousness that assistance is greatly required, as the timing, in your terms, of conception, growth and birth, is of the utmost importance.

The passage into Earth consciousness is mathematically programmed. It is energetically understood, from our framework of existence, very precisely. Should you have the capability to understand our reasoning behind this process, it would not be inaccurate to say that this can be plotted. Entry into the dense physical state is subject to energetic emanations from the stars and the planets. As you approach and pass through your own solar system, the density of your being increases enormously, and it is this point of entry where guidance and assistance are most required by the incoming spiritual being. The planets that you pass close to, which you interpenetrate, all have a bearing on who you are. This does not mean to say that they are influential in your life, it merely means that they are a contributory factor to your psycho-emotional state in the dense matter that you know as the body, giving you certain characteristics, a defined personality, which you will endure for a fixed period of time. Each planet has a different energy, a different emotional quality, and the planets within your solar system can be said to have certain aspects of these attributes, particularly as they are part of your influencing environment. Therefore each movement of these planets, while you are in your physical being, can have an effect on your emotional body.

Astrology has the ability to reveal the possibility of how this occurs and what this means in your life. Do understand, however, that within the solar system you are actually free from influence, but what you experience is the change in energy and the shift in focus, not only as it affects you but every other individual on the surface of the planet.

Consequently you react, sometimes in an irrational way, until a sympathetic environment is recreated within the solar system, one that is compatible with your own vibratory frequency. Do understand that this affects your energetic body, not your physical body. Your energetic body creates the physical body. Everything contained within the energetic body has physical manifestations. Consequently, the memory contained within the chromosomes, the genes, the DNA structure itself, is actually contained energetically in your aura, hence the ability to maintain a consistency and flow of information through time, allowing you to maintain influence and continuity.

Remember, nothing is lost and nothing is wasted. In your terms, as you grow in light, it is as though the tunnel of entry through the solar system becomes wider, allowing you to have access to that which is without, enabling you – in your terms – to channel, to be aware, to be instinctive, to be intuitive, to allow yourselves to know what you have already experienced beyond your body, beyond your solar system, where there is all. As your tunnel widens, you therefore have potential access to all. However, the density of your being, particularly your conscious mind, means that this will not always come in a rush but what you (as we have observed), feel is a sense of knowing even though you cannot voice it. Sometimes, what you cannot voice is secret, cannot be revealed. Sometimes, this feeling is sufficient as this energetic response can communicate itself to the rest of your physical being, allowing it to awaken, to sense its security within the universe. It gives your psycho-emotional being a sense of belonging, of safety, of purpose and a sense of destiny. It allows you real communication because you understand; it is part of who you are and where you come from, and it gives you, with your enquiring mind, the ability to send impulses to this understanding, to become know-ledge, to speak it, to put it into practical operation. This is who you really are.

Becoming Light Bodies

The structure of the DNA itself is being awakened to its cosmic potential. The DNA is nearing the end of its func-tionality as there is limited energy, limited memory to which it can respond owing to its density of being. The point in time will be reached when literally the physical body will start to glow; and turn into an energetic glowing vibrancy, which is easier to equate with dematerialisation while still being visible. This is where the point of evolution is reached, where you no longer are dense beings of physical shape and form. You become finer beings of light, colour and tonality who, whilst still maintaining shape, have the opportunity to transmigrate, to allow your consciousness to be in another place in whatever shape, form and density required by your spiritual blueprint. So close is that time to the now, it naturally means that in your time much adjustment and fine-tuning have to take place to allow the DNA within your physical structure to resonate at a new frequency. This puts greater stress on some of the protein structures within the DNA that have not been stressed previously, alerting you to needs which go beyond your conscious capacity. We observe people becoming aware, sensitive, experiencing aspects of being not previously encountered on such a large scale before, driving individuals to seek answers – from situations, people, or from reading books – where they would never have looked normally, as they seek clarification of what is happening to them.

A lot of effort has been employed to establish the reality of spirit as being viable and real. As science is unable to measure or perceive this reality, it has been achieved in other ways. What is happening within your reality is that this aspect of your being, this means of transferring information, is being totally by-passed. People – as this is an age for you to be responsible – are awakening to what you call Christ consciousness in the world, at this moment. You have evolved.

There is no need for a martyr, for a guru or a Master. That time has passed. You are on your own. You must seek, on your own. You must ask questions, on your own. You must learn to formulate in your minds the right questions, as without the right questions the correct answers cannot be given, which is why you often receive silence in response to questioning. You have reached a time when, as your material world is beginning to disintegrate, you can no longer equate who you are in relation to something that is fading and crumbling. You then have to decide in your own mind to what, or to which, you need now to relate. The choice is yours. You are free to decide. But do understand that you work in co-operation with other forces within the universe who are endeavouring to alert you to a need, so that you may respond.

Understand that, as you mature at the level of spirit, there are other realities to pursue and that there is life, as you understand it, beyond your own psycho-emotional, spiritual cycle. You are an example of what is possible, which is why it is important that you succeed, but succeed in realisation, in allowing yourselves to be. Within you is everything. In everything there is all that is. God. The mother-father vibration. The encapsulation. The essence of truth. The 'is'.

Owing to the spatial rearrangement on the physical surface of your Earth, you will learn to use technology in a way that can maintain your life and that has not been used previously. This will enable you to live below the earth, submerged beneath your oceans and suspended beyond your atmosphere. As your spiritual reality alerts you to these possibilities, you will enjoy radical, physical change to enable this to take place. There will be less need for physical mobility, and the density of your bones will decrease. The elasticity of your muscles, your tendons, your ligaments, will increase, allowing you greater flexibility of movement. Your nervous system will become more vibrant and will undergo some physical enlargement in certain aspects of the body, notably the point between the eyes above the top of the nose, below the left lung as it connects into the spleen, extending from the thymus around the thymus, not into the thymus, as though the thymus itself is being placed within a stronger energetic structure.

New Lands

There are also those beings already on the Earth who are not part of our reality, who will assist wherever it is practically necessary to enable you to facilitate radical change. You may not come to know them well. It is almost as though help will suddenly appear, assist and then disappear. You will be guided. You will be assisted at many levels. Within the next one hundred years there will be a crack in the earth – it is difficult for us to accurately describe – forty degrees west of your point zero longitude, which will have significant repercussions in Western Europe and the coast of Africa. In turn, this will cause sympathetic reactions around the world. Notably in the centre of what is now South America, and also within the eastern part of the United States and Canada, tracing a line from the Sea of Oil in South America (the Gulf of Maracaibo in Venezuela where there is great oil production and pollution) northwards to the Great Bay within Canada. This will also allow a resurgence of land to occur south of the Equator, east of where we now have Indonesia, giving forth new land, new vitality, new mineral configurations.

There will be, in your terms, a radical reduction of population, hence the need in the now for people to reach a state of awareness, as they will be the ones who, in future time, will perpetuate life on the surface of the Earth and within. There are those who will be sufficiently evolved to accept transmigration as a possibility and put it into actuality, who will allow themselves to be elevated from within the Earth, to be taken directly to other dimensions, to be able to convey, teach and enlighten those who work in co-operation, to explain the emotional state and what is needed, what is required, and how this may be put into effect.

Within the next thousand years your energetic transformation will largely be complete. This will allow you to be the energy of who you are, allowing you to accept the consciousness of your being, bringing into alignment the amnesia state of spirit in physical consciousness, so that you exist in all dimensions at the same time. This will bring to a conclusion the spiritual, psycho-emotional evolutionary state of your development. It will allow you to be catapulted once more through time, to take on board your birthright as an evolving form of consciousness that is moving through space, through time, towards understanding of other levels, other frameworks of existence; assisting where possible, partaking where you feel is most appropriate.

As one door shuts, another opens. As one reality reaches its point – the apex of its potential development – it then comes into total consciousness, into total understanding of its being at every possible level. That vibration, that energy permeating through the whole physical framework of the universe, may be absorbed and used by others who seek that practical explanation, who need to feel, in your terms, that evolvement has been completed, thereby giving them the courage, the desire, the will and, indeed, the love to succeed.

It is a very dense individual who cannot sense change of the magnitude that you are experiencing. There will be those who seek clarification of the change, and there will be those who seek to ignore what this change represents. The previous decade, as you experienced it, was an enormous indulgence of dependence, of denial of selfhood. The effect of that is so enormous that it is being experienced within your own time. So special is this time. Should this have occurred perhaps at the beginning of the current century, you would not have experienced the effect so quickly. Such is the magnetism and clarity of energy within your environment that any such major denial that is put into action by you will return with great force and with much speed. This necessitates that each individual be in touch with their need and be prepared to take responsibility for making sure that this is executed with diligence and integrity. There is no sense of judgement here, merely that you will no longer be able to deny who you are. No longer will you be able to live under a false guise, or disguise. The superficial framework in which many of those in your society place themselves as an energetic form will be impossible to create owing to the intensity of the vibration that is permeating your Earth. As the century closes and the new millennium begins you will reach a point when it will be difficult to perpetuate falsehood. If this is what you are experiencing, everybody bar none will come to know and experience what this means.

The matters that we speak of can only accurately be

contained within the reality from which they are given. The impact that you receive upon your mind is not sufficient to explain in actuality the evolving process. We speak merely to alert you to the momentous change that will take place. As the core of your Earth's being is attracting towards itself its own lines of consciousness or tunnels through your solar system, it is causing cracks or fissures, energetic fissures within its own surface, which will alert it to the changes, the physical manipulations that it needs to exert on itself, to maintain its own life being.

You will recognise, when the time comes, the reasoning behind this as you will be able to read the structures within the Earth correctly and use the messages and the energies that are contained within it with responsibility. There is much hidden within your Earth's surface that was placed within it aeons ago to allow you to have access to it when the time is right.

In many respects your crop circles are physical manifestations of the tunnels of energy that are entering the Earth for the Earth's own consciousness. They are mathematical imprints of these energy tunnels, enabling the Earth itself to draw towards it what it needs, allowing it to experience its own evolution through consciousness.

We are merely saying that this is a time of responsibility for you, and you will come to find, to see, to use and to understand those structures, those energies, those revelations that will be given to you. But understand that you will have reached a point of wisdom where they can be put to constructive use by those who have learnt and understood.

If this is the case, if this is how things are for you, if you are capable of being responsible to such a degree, please look at yourselves now, and understand who you are, how far you have come, and the metaphorical distance that you have travelled to allow you to embrace and take on board concepts beyond your understanding and knowledge. But remember that knowledge is not a limitation for understanding.

The structures that are being given to you to visualise are allowing you to evoke within yourselves what you feel is to come. Know who you are. Do not be afraid to be who you are, as you are becoming something else. We can merely say there is much support and love which is an energy within which we play – being given to you to enable you to see, and to offer you the courage to experience and the clarity to see. It is because of who you are that you can receive what is given. Be discerning. Accept only what you feel is appropriate. That is all you need, but know you accept far more than you know. As your hearts and your minds become fused as one, you will draw towards you everything within the void, within which is contained everything.

We applaud who you are. We acknowledge, with love, your search for truth. This is who you are. This is what you do. You will succeed. You may not come to know all, but you will understand all with love, allowing, in your own wisdom, to be clearer within your operational selves.

Once again, focus your mind within the red energetic rod. Draw your mind away, consciously bring it back into your head, making it part of your own vibration once more. See the image in the centre of the circle gradually fade, knowing that you take with it the essence of what it is and what it represents. Be within yourself for a moment as we withdraw and leave a register of our vibration in your heart. As we pass, sense the passing within the heart itself.

FOUR

Your Journey Through the Solar System

*Visualise, if you will, an energetic mesh in the centre of a circle.
This mesh undulates like a wave. The mesh is highly intricate.
View it as a carpet. View it as a golden white wave. See it
undulating above the circle. Conceptualise this in whatever way
you wish. There are concentrations of red nodes at some of the
intersections within the mesh structure. Feel, or see, a vacuum-
like edifice emanating from the four corners of the mesh, escalating
upwards, that reflects silver-yellow. The upward momentum of
this energy will create a force-field that will allow your mind to be
drawn into a reality not of this place. Allow yourself to sense the
change, as this affects the vibratory state of your mind. Once
again, we restate that each time you visualise an energetic
structure, it adds to what you have already created through
visualising the earlier energy-structures, enabling you to move
with greater freedom, to access consciousness at other levels now
available to you.*

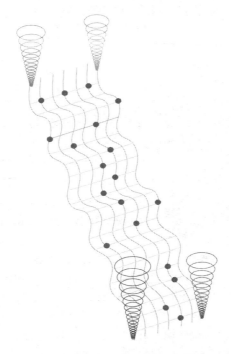

We are now at one. We have reached the point where we have discussed constitutional elements and structure within the physicality of your own being, and how they affect your position on the Earth within the physical framework of the universe. We have discussed the minerals and trace elements that you have within the physicality of your body; how they energetically connect with the energy of the Earth; how this energetic structure permeates outwards into the cosmos itself providing potential connections with other forms of being within it. We have set the parameters that will stretch you to a point when the physicality of the body is made redundant.

We would now like to say that the elements contained within the physical body are connecting you energetically to various other points within the physical framework of the universe, until you reach the state when you will become a free-floating energy form that can maintain itself in an energetic structure of less density. Until that point is reached, there will be a need for you to contain within you – constitutionally – these trace elements, minerals and organic compositions in their correct proportions. As we talk about the elements, about each having a life, a structure, a sense of continuum, all energetic continuum within the framework of the universe, we also would like to indicate the potential combustibility and consequences that emanate from the coming together of elements in an unstable situation.

We wish to talk about radiation and the long-term effect this has on your planet through the unnatural combination of elements and the processes of bringing them together or reducing them to half-lives, to different states. It is emitting a tremendous power that is beyond your capacity to control, and it affects not only the physical structure of your Earth, but also, as it emanates outwards, your solar system.

Understand that the creation of radioactive energy is unleashing a primordial force that goes beyond the capability of your planet to contain. It creates an energetic resonance within the physical framework of the Earth that causes a dissolution of the energetic support mechanisms within the physicality of the Earth's core itself. If this radioactivity was placed within a group of living cells, it would cause these cells to collapse in upon themselves, thereby sucking away the life-force and the memory that represented this group's cellular consciousness.

In many ways, within the physical framework of the Earth, the same situation is created which takes away the memory and the potential of the physical structures within the Earth, because the Earth, like your own psychological, emotional selves, is evolving. By removing the memory, by taking away that sense of precognition of where it is heading, you are, in effect, denying progression. More importantly, by taking away the memory, you are taking away viability of survival.

1995 – 2045

Over the next 50 years, in your time, you will experience – within the surface structure of your Earth – your land caving in on itself in areas where there have been strong emissions of radioactive activity. These activities weaken the layering effect within the Earth's structure, creating fissures or cracks, which will allow subterranean levels to communicate with each other, causing friction through movement, which increases the potential for major earth movement and will bring about, deep within the Earth, quakes which will affect the ratio between land and sea, thereby altering the bedrock of society in which you live. The energetic ramifications that permeate your solar system can be equally destructive.

There will also be much more volcanic activity in unexpected places as subterranean movement is going to unleash weaknesses within structures of the Earth itself, causing spontaneous combustion from beneath the oceans and, to a lesser extent, within the land itself. Some of these have already been plotted and are expected. But so great is some of the movement within the Earth, and because movement is being accelerated at an unexpected level, it will create a disturbance that is unexpected. The time frame of some of these major eruptions can be contained within the next 40 years, the acceleration of which will come after approximately 25 years' time.

We will now talk about your emotional being as it responds and corresponds to the planets within your solar system. If there is a correspondence in this way, then any energetic emanation that comes from the Earth and causes disturbance within the solar system, is also going to have an effect on your emotional being. As this radiomagnetic active by–product is consistent in its emanation, it sets up an increasing magnetic field that leaves the Earth like a wave pattern and comes through the atmosphere of your solar system. This means that the delicate energy balance, through the energy corridors that we have already discussed, is altered, thereby diminishing both the structure within which the Earth is held and also the channels of communication themselves. The result is comparable to an imposed sense of isolation owing to strong energy impulses coming from the earth itself through which co-operative communication is not always able to penetrate.

In effect, what we are saying is that the possibility to create a force-field or a shield around the Earth which is impermeable to outside help, is actually possible. What you are experiencing at the moment is that, in various isolated areas on the surface of the Earth, this condition is already being created. If this continues in a global sense you will reach the stage when co-operation – our ability to comm-unicate and pass on practical information, our accessibility being present on the Earth – becomes so diminished as to be-come virtually impossible. Should this state ever be created, it would mean that you are totally isolated from the rest of the universe, and it is only through your own efforts that you may possibly extricate yourselves from any difficulty that may arise.

When we talk of potential for annihilation it is this that we speak of, which is largely due to your own bodies of government and science to explore; an energy over which they cannot exercise control. They are blinkered to understand the total ramifications of what they create. You have movements within your sociological and political structures which have an ability to sense the inappropriateness of developing such an energy. This appeals to your primal sense of survival and should be listened to. This particular energy combination is one that is rarely used, because once it is instigated it is not actually possible to reverse the process. That is true in our dimension and, as we observe, is also true within all the realities that we have had contact with. As you live on a dense structure the damage that can be inflicted, therefore, can be enormous.

You already experience how the physical body reacts when it comes into contact with such an energetic force. If this is part of the microcosmic reaction, allow your minds to extend that reaction into the universe, for we say it does not stop in and around the Earth, it extends outwards and interferes with a very delicate network of communication which is actually part of your life support mechanism. As you are only beginning to understand what this may mean, you are ignorant of the effect that is being caused. The basis on which your governments and science base the efficacy and practicality of this use is grossly misguided and is exercised or rather, has been worked, purely for economic gain. Within the illusion of your sociological and political reality it has been given life perpetuation to justify its existence, which is incorrect. It is being made to perpetuate because no one can stop it.

We would also like to discuss the practical use of radiation to treat abnormal growths within the physicality of the body. As we have already described, this energy, this quality of energy, in our terms, is vacuous – it draws energy from, as well as generating energy towards, something else. As this is placed within the physicality of the body, it draws energy from the cells so they collapse upon each other, and die, in your terms. There is no longer energy present. The delicate web of your energetic form, therefore, is interfered with. It artificially raises the vibration of your energetic body which puts a strain not only on the physical but also on the emotional and psychological state of your being. It also creates an abnormal resonance in and around your physicality which displaces spiritual contact and creates a feeling of dissociation and isolation from your very source-cells. This does not mean that you are left unsupported and abandoned; it merely means that as you have the ability to feel and sense the spiritual reality, this ability is virtually obliterated until this resonance, this abnormal resonance, ceases to be.

However, people rarely recover from this abnormal resonance that is introduced in their psycho-emotional being. This means that as you all are, indeed, as we all are caught in a multi-faceted way of communication, that you yourselves, as a result, become encased within a bubble that tends to isolate you from the network, producing feelings of anxiety (as we observe them) and in some cases, loss of self. We do not judge as to whether this should be used to prolong life or not. We merely present a proposition as to the effect it causes. To clarify; when it is used in extreme, the effect which that can have on the Earth-body itself and as a result on your solar system and the whole of your galaxy, is felt and experienced within the whole of the universal galaxy.

Understand also that as science and industry continue to pollute the natural environment and habitat in which you live, this too is absorbed within the Earth. If we look at the seas and at the abnormal combinations of elements that are being placed within the sea, these eventually precipitate. If the precipitates are heavy, they not only fall to the ocean floor, but are absorbed by the sub-aquatic Earth floor. As the surface of your Earth changes and some of the land that is currently under the sea re-emerges into the open air, you must understand and appreciate that there will be areas of land that will be unable to propagate natural growth within the flora aspect of your world for some time, as the density of the material that covers the earth will form an impenetrable layer thereby limiting communication of air, water, sun and all the primordial life-forces, thereby denying soil the ability to generate life.

The descriptions we use are simplistic. Understand the implications can often be more serious. The Earth itself is, in some ways, aware of these imbalances and this is being communicated to the Earth. There are forces, not of your Earth but surrounding your Earth, who materialise themselves sufficiently to enter your atmosphere. Once within this environment they are projecting dense energy structures into the Earth's surface, not only creating a force-field but also markers, so that as and when the Earth begins to rotate on its axis, these markers will connect with other markers outside your atmospheric environment, enabling it to fit or place itself within a new energetic structure.

The change in seasons, the climatic variables that you are experiencing on the Earth's surface, is largely part of the preparation for the change. A new magnetic field is being put into place to facilitate this change, as this magnetism itself – it would not be inaccurate to say – has a heat. The whole of the Earth as a result will be experiencing what this heat means to it. This heat is being caused by the friction of the withdrawal of one energetic magnetic force-field and the input of a new force-field, creating a contra-flow which, in your terms, can be experienced as a raising of temperature. Once the withdrawal and the input have been completed, the friction will no longer be present, and the earth will be allowed to adjust to its own natural seasons, as you experience them.

But understand that as this new magnetic structure is of a high-energy quality, the consciousness it supports will be more highly evolved, largely, than what you have at present, which gives greater clarification to the idea of separation we have described earlier. Spiritually this is understood, and you are preparing, adapting and accepting what has been put into motion. We say this so that you understand once more that there is no judgement, that certain aspects of culture, society or race are not being singled out above another. There is no ultimate separation. At the spiritual and cosmic level there is complete co-operation and understanding.

Cosmic Influences

It is appropriate at this time to look objectively at your entry from outside your solar system, and then through the solar system to become incarnate within the Earth. The paths that you choose to take through the stars have a certain application and resonance of their own which alert the memory of the incarnating consciousness to who it is and what it means to be. As this consciousness enters the solar system from the galaxy it acquires yet greater density. The solar system adds the memory of your emotional being to the consciousness that is already represented. Your pathway through the magnetism of various planets will, therefore, give you certain characteristics that, emotionally, will be manifest in different ways thereby taking on a guise, a personality, a suit of clothes, that make you recognisable for who you are and distinct from everybody else.

Understand that the closer you pass to a particular planet, the greater influence that will have on an aspect of your personality. Each of you has a greater affinity to one particular planet than another. If you move outwards into the galaxy, then into your Milky Way, and into all star systems within your galaxy, your point of entries are different. Consequently, the cosmic attractability that you have towards certain stars is very particular. The more you can identify yourselves with these planets and stars the easier it will be to understand the nature of your being.

It is not necessarily that you come from another place, it is merely that there is an input into your consciousness as you travel close to certain stars and certain planets, giving you a blueprint for incarnation. This naturally enhances what you already genetically have within your physical body.

Understand this: it is your energetic body that creates your physical body, and as a result, the DNA structure is merely a physical representation of what is already contained within the energetic body. As your energetic body is consciousness, soul and spirit, as your soul is cosmic, as you have unlimited access within the framework of the universe, that memory therefore is enhanceable, giving you a particular make-up, allowing you to attract towards you certain experiences you need to endure, to allow understanding to be evoked. This is where the Buddhist philosophy largely comes from, and it is closely allied to what you understand as karma.

As your energetic consciousness leaves the solar system and enters specifically the gravitational aspect of your Earth, it will descend and approach the mathematical co-ordinates it has chosen as a point of entry into the Earth itself. It is at this point that the influence of your parents becomes real, as this incoming consciousness senses again the cosmic stickiness that emanates from the mind of the parents, and is drawn towards it. Having connected with the correct co-ordinates, consciousness then waits for the appropriate physical circumstances to occur to allow it to enter the dense physical body within the womb, and it is at the point of conception that this occurs. It is not appropriate to try and create a difference between soul and consciousness. In your terms they must be associated as one. It is part of the same energetic force.

As this consciousness enters physicality it interpenetrates the Earth through these energy corridors which become a natural part of the incarnating being. When consciousness becomes fully vibrant in physical form, the new Earth-being maintains contact with the rest of the solar system, the galaxy and the universe, through these energetic corridors it used when it first entered the Earth. Cosmic communication is naturally present.

You can use these energy corridors just by knowing they are there and knowing you have free access to them within your own personal energetic corridors. If there is a particular energetic corridor that you wish to place yourself in, trust and know that all that is required is for you to project your mind so that you feel secure within it. You have free access to use them at your discretion. We merely advise that you first have some understanding of why you need to use them at any given point in time. That is all.

As we trace these corridors outwards into the solar system, we find that, at certain points, these corridors are sealed. Likewise, as you leave the solar system and go into the galaxies themselves, this forms a protection so that you are not at liberty to make contact with any higher consciousness form before you are capable of tolerating that reality. Within the solar system, as you mature and grow older, as you experience life, some of these partitions dissolve, allowing you to extend outwards to a more evolved sense of being, a greater sense of Self. Understand that the planets do not influence, the planets, in your terms, add character and personality. As you progress through life, as you mature, as you accept your spiritual reality, you then have the potential to dissolve these partitions at a more evolved emotional stage. Each of the solar planets corresponds to particular emotional states. They influence your being, but only as they have helped create your being, not as they have control over your being, and as you progress emotionally through your solar planets you begin to liberate yourselves totally from their influence, giving you the opportunity to become cosmic in part, to be able to have conscious awareness of your place within the physical framework of the cosmos.

As you leave the solar system itself, you lose the need of dependence, of having to rely on emotion as a means of creating growth and experiencing life. As you leave the solar system and enter into the galaxies, you then become the complete spiritual, psychological, emotional being you are. You are able to consciously take on board your birthright. You are able, largely, as much as it is possible, to remember who you are. As you return once more to connect with the cosmic impulses, you are also able to look more objectively on your being, on your reality, and on your place in life through time. It is to this end that you work, to understand the cosmic soul. The spiritual soul is merely contained within the psycho-emotional body – it reflects only your growth through the solar system.

It would seem appropriate at this time to refrain from enlarging further on this state, as there is a natural conclusion to what has been explained. As you are cosmic, as you are becoming cosmic, so we are cosmic. When you become consciousness itself there will be no stopping point once you leave the galaxies to enter through the solar system on to the Earth. It is as though there is straight passage. But as the Earth becomes pure energetic consciousness as well, the effect this has within the solar system as a result, will mean that they, themselves, will become consciousness. So the density of their creating influence will no longer be present, freeing the solar system itself into its own natural cosmic being, providing an integration with the galaxy you live on, to allow this experience to be communicated through time and space.

We are here to serve. We are here to evoke intelligence, to allow you to find your own way to your own truth, to the one wisdom that each and every one of you has contained within yourselves. It is with much – it is difficult to describe – excitement that we feel we can communicate in such an available way, in a way that has never been feasible before. This, in many respects, is a compliment to you, that you can accept and indeed find, the place from where we speak. If you are capable of doing that, your application of what you understand and know is limitless. We do experience love, though not in the emotional context. You have a term, the word unconditional, which largely describes what we experience. It is within this pure vibration that we live. It is this on which we depend as a sense of, in your terms, joy, that allows us to feel in many respects the need to communicate.

Never underestimate your power. Never try to devalue what you instinctively know. It is rooted in a very solid core of consciousness which is who you are and extends right through the universe. It is this that you are discovering within yourselves. Enjoy your journey. Be alert to your needs, and respond as you feel appropriate.

Project your mind once more into the energetic net. Feel, or acknowledge, or see, the place where you left your mind. The energetic vacuum is being lifted, leaving you free-standing on the net itself. Gradually draw back your mind to yourself, so that you become one with your own density of being. We withdraw our energy and dissolve the net, until the next time.

FIVE

Exploring the Mind

Visualise, if you will, an equilateral triangle, standing vertically, with one side on the floor. Imagine a verticle circle bisecting the two base points, so you see a semi-circular bulge emanating downwards from the base of the triangle. Place your vision on the apex of the triangle, as though you are looking down the slope to the point where the base of the triangle is in contact with the floor.

Place, as best you can within your visualisation, another triangle near the point where the equilateral triangle has contact with the floor, so the angle of degree will be 30 degrees of the new triangle, as it sits on top of the first and its contact with the floor. The detail is not vital for you to know, we use it for illustrative purposes.

So you have one triangle crossing another at the point where the first triangle touches the floor. Place your mind in the semi-circle as it bisects the base of the equilateral triangle; as though you are looking down towards its point, or apex, as it would be if it were standing upright. The two triangles create a magnetism that interlocks with the structures within which you have previously placed yourself. The bisecting piece of the circle, as it has contact with the equilateral triangle, provides an environment of movement, to allow the mind to adjust its frequency in direct ratio to your tolerability of this vibration.

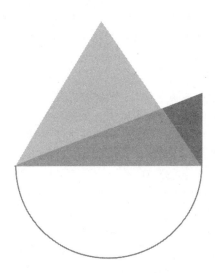

Again, understand that as you place your mind within this configuration, you automatically bring with you the memory of what you have previously created. You are, therefore, enmeshed in a highly intricate mathematical theorem which has direct bearing to our origin within our galaxy. Each subsequent energetic visualisation we will give, will allow you to focus more clearly on our origin and its location.

Understand that as you are connected through energetic corridors to your universe, your mind automatically travels through these corridors in your journeys of exploration. To have contact with consciousness form as we are, it is necessary for you to create an artificial corridor to allow yourself to travel through space-time, to have greater familiarity of who we are, and with each visualisation, allowing you to experience a greater attention and absorption of what we represent. By the end of these communications you will have an automatic, albeit artificial, connection with this consciousness we have been for you, and you will unconsciously resonate with what it represents. As a result, what we have spoken of can be reinstituted within your mind, to be put into vibrant, conscious knowledge, knowing that because of the structure you have created you can appreciate the understanding that has potential for knowledge.

We now wish to talk about the mind. For a moment, close your eyes and focus your mind in this semi-circle energy formation. Allow your mind to absorb whatever is present, and understand that your mind is being alerted to its final evolution as it will be. Understand also that it is only your mind outside the density of your being that can understand and appreciate what this means. Within the density of your being, it is not possible for it to convey what this represents. The adjustment is made, and absorption has begun.

Within the physical structure of your body, inside the cranial cavity, you have a gelatinous mass which you understand is the brain. It provides a means for you to be a thinking being. It is a highly evolved structure which is little understood by your science as it presently exists. Understand that you only utilise approximately 3% of its potential, and that you are coming to a time when the genetic memory contained within the brain will gradually allow you to evoke what its potential means and how it can be used. The full potential of your brain will only be used when you become consciousness itself. It will not allow you to tolerate the complexity or the weight of understanding that is possible within the density of your being. This must be confined within your conscious day-to-day basis of living. The daily basis of your living will never be able to represent true mind-in-action until it becomes pure consciousness.

We wish you to visualise the brain in three sections: the left, the right, and the back. They have three distinct and separate dynamic actions: the left is for conscious application, the right is for unconscious application, and the base rear is connected with universal application. Therefore universal application applies itself to both aspects, stimulating conscious and unconscious in the moment; communicating impulses that can be received consciously and put into action, and those impulses received unconsciously which cannot be tolerated by the rational consciousness and stored, ready to be put to use at a later date. There are tiny bridges connecting left and right. Understand that the bridges, the crossover points, have a greater density in energetic terms than the two separate cortex centres. As you evolve through time, you seek to achieve an ability to receive consciously and unconsciously simultaneously.

Once you have acquired this potential, the bridges separating left and right acquire the density of the rear base cortex. In practical terms you become an instinctive, immediate and responsive vibratory being who works and absorbs at all levels instantaneously, you feel, think, know and react within the same impulse; there is a totality, a universal connection which allows you to receive the complete picture of any concept that is within your magnetic area.

You have reached a point of evolution when you are, figuratively speaking, developing the muscle of the left and right brain as it connects with the rear base; so you allow yourselves to feed spasmodically on the left side from the rear base in minute bursts. Clarification and confirmation are given by impulses that come from the right to the left sides of the brain, allowing you to feel what you know is correct, understanding that the right side, in many respects, is developing at a more rapid rate. But also, as all three centres of the brain have an area of magnetism that is special to themselves, this will automatically influence the others. So we are creating a picture of the interdependence and complementary nature of how, at a very basic level, the cerebral cortices communicate with each other. The illustration is crude, but it suffices to explain what we relate.

As you are part of the emotional spiritual cycle, the right brain can communicate to your feeling aspect what this represents to you. It gives you clarification of your spiritual reality. It allows you to conceptualise the God-source. It allows you to appreciate Christ-ing and what this means to you. It allows you to sense your path through your own individual evolutionary process. At this time, what is less developed is the left brain, which allows universality to convey itself – you may call it cosmic objectivity to transmit practical knowledge so that it is immediately available to be used by the conscious brain.

This is the area where you are now knocking on the door, where somehow within yourselves intelligence is evoking itself, to allow you to conceptualise the possibility of you absorbing and reacting in this way, to be able to take on board extraordinary concepts which are beyond your Earth knowledge, understanding them, and putting them into practice. You have been injected with fear which anaesthetised your ability to accept this part of who you are. Like all anaesthetics, it has a limited time of operation and this anaesthetising effect is now beginning to subside. This means that, in the framework of your own lifetime, you will have to come to accept the uniqueness and extraordinary nature of your very being as it relates within the physical framework of the universe.

This goes beyond any sense of spiritual communion or communication and takes you into a whole new area. You have a place within the universe outside of this time-space and you all have, within you, experience of what this means. You have wisdom derived from experience within these realms which is naturally contained within your genetic memory. As you strive, spiritually, you take on board that divine vibration of increasing intensity which stimulates right brain activity, which allows universality, and the opportunity through increased magnetism – to thereby communicate more directly with the left brain. Allowing it to accept, in actual fact, what it is.

Your greatest difficulty is in accepting who you are. You have reached, through time, a level of maturity, allowing spiritual realisation to be. This frees potential to make the quantum leap into cosmic consciousness itself, allowing the left brain to expand into knowledge, knowing that having experienced this out of time, your own wisdom will alert you to the vibrancy of what this means in your psycho-emotional, spiritual representation within the framework of the cosmos.

Cosmic Consciousness

We wish to stress, or wish to divert, your attention to the fact that your soul is cosmic. You have, in many ways, grown up. You have the facility to accept the possibility that the psycho-emotional, spiritual cycle is not the sole cycle within which you are contained. There are greater and more expansive cycles through time which are in operation. Your own spiritual maturity will make sure that you have the confidence and the application to be able to deal with what this means. We have a situation here where we try to voice, or communicate, something that goes beyond the density of words, which is why the analogies we draw for you are often crude and inappropriate in our terms. This is why it is necessary for your mind at another level to have contact with who we are, to allow your subconscious right brain to absorb the understanding, so that this will be evoked into more left-brain conscious knowledge at a later date as your evolutionary development finds an appropriate time to make this a viable proposition.

The Earth does not have a soul as you understand it. It does have an energetic counterpart elsewhere within your galaxy, and it is this that it is drawing towards itself. There are those who can work with this energetic counterpart and feed it. This other consciousness that feeds it cannot approach the Earth directly, however, owing to its density of being. It has a counterpart. It is part of a divine plan. It doesn't have a psycho-emotional state as you have, but it is part of the whole and there is no separation between who you are and what it represents.

You are part of a very unique period where all realities, as they are opened to you, are coming in to surround you, and make themselves available for you, should you wish to enquire as to who they are and what they represent.

Some of you already have the ability to experience counter-time, time between time, flashes of other realities which are coming into consciousness. Crudely speaking, being in two places at once. Within your density of being, it is as though the time clock is beginning to deteriorate and dissolve, and you are becoming able to experience yourselves through time. This may not be voiced in words, but the feeling, the experience, the sense of knowing is there. It is knowing who you are, what you have been and knowing what you will become.

Some of you, because you are part of aspects of consciousness that are secret, or contained from others, will be unable to voice some of what you feel. Some of you are part of consciousness that is going to evolve into different timespaces, to work with the Earth – and at more distant, less dense, vibratory levels. And you are beginning to feel the weight of responsibility as you become aware of what is coming forward from the future into the present. You cannot voice it but the feeling is there – the feeling of having to do something enormous which seems totally outside your capacity to facilitate its happening. You are merely being alerted to some super-future state. But as those time barriers dissolve, you vibrate more freely within the energetic corridors of your being, absorbing the nature of your reality; not only being alerted to your purpose in this life, but your destiny as your purpose is projected into future time.

A Christ-ing is the ultimate vibration within the physical density of your being. It is the Christ-ing that is evolving the uniqueness of who you are. Accept this. Sometimes there is a courage that is needed which you feel you do not have. Our understanding of feeling is limited, but as we appreciate it, the spiritual vibration – which is a very part of your nature – will allow this courage to be maintained so that it comes from beyond the density of being that you experience in the physical body, but is still part of your cycle, your emotional spiritual make-up. As you bring memory from the spiritual state genetically into the physical presence, it is that change in memory, that change of tonality, of vibration, of frequency, which will raise you into a state where this is possible. This will all be in place once the final emotional hurdle of maturity has been reached.

There are beings within the physical environment of the Earth who are reaching a point when the erotic desire to maintain consciousness in physical form becomes redundant, and that physical form will be removed to create space for a greater intensity of vibration. This happens in two ways. First, co-operation with a cosmic being while the physical form is still vibrant. This highly evolved spiritual being offers, through co-operation, to exchange the physical body with the cosmic being, to allow it to experience a more intense observation of the Earth reality so that this may be conveyed more directly to like-minded vibrations of like consciousness. The departing spirit yields itself finally to being within spiritual consciousness itself, and works within this realm to assist and facilitate a continuation of the Christing. The cosmic being has little difficulty in maintaining the life vitality of the physical body and can utilise the energy of the mind-impulse from the brain, and draw on a greater percentage of operability of that brain, to maintain its own life support mechanism within a greater density. For those who can see, if you regard a take-over in this manner, there will be one light emanating from the physical body but there will be no reflection or light emanation of an emotional state. That emotional state is part of an energetic experience that passes with the co-operating spiritual being and goes into that energetic memory which becomes part of spirit itself. So you have the irrational situation of a physical body that does not experience the emotional state. It is not subject to the denser laws of your reality.

There are many who have co-operated in this way, and there are therefore many who maintain life on Earth in an artificial situation. There are those now who are identifying themselves as being who they are. The momentum of this will gather force as those among you can come to accept the possibility of this phenomenon. There are those cosmic beings who themselves take on a gross density and walk around the Earth to partake in the psycho-emotional state without being able to enjoy it at the level that you appreciate it. These beings are not very prevalent, have little influence, but can be intrusive and disturbing. They seek to manipulate and to be powerful, to validate their being and to acquire greater influence. Because of the nature of who they are, this is not possible within the density of being in relation to the cosmic experience, and is not possible within the density of your Earth. But do understand that as you, as light-beings, work in co-operation with other theoretical light-beings, this desire to acquire power will not be achieved. Your very uniqueness of being will allow you to enjoy the glory of your world.

Presently, as you bring down to the Earth various forms of consciousness and high vibrational states, it is as though you are creating a pressure on the Earth itself. This is creating a form of chaos. Understand, however, that chaos can acquire a level of density that will then make a leap into consciousness itself, causing radical change within the psychology of your being, allowing your mind to accept the vibrancy of who you are: spirit, mind, and body, acting as one within the cosmos.

There is a mathematical law here which has been proven within your science that focuses on chaos in this way, but understand that all discoveries do, in effect, relate to the physical machinations of the mind and consciousness. Everything is energy, and energy behaves and reacts in the same way at that level of its density of being. As your theoretical mathematicians and physicists conceptualise, they are actually expressing the working of consciousness itself. This is not how they regard their work. It is, however, how things are.

We are saying, therefore, that you are fast approaching the time when you will make that leap in consciousness into higher consciousness and accept the glory of your being as it is, and as it will be within the cosmos. We are aware that we factually describe matters as we see them. We have a level of understanding that this may be regarded by you in a darker aspect than it is given. We are merely describing the reality. We are indicating that each and every one of you has a power that you are only coming to understand, and that within this personal power there are no limits to what you can facilitate and achieve.

We wish to say that if you are unable to accept the glory of your being, you will not be able to accept reality as it is evolving. As your psycho-emotional selves are hurling towards a catharsis in time, you can no longer depend on your past experience to indicate what is coming your way. That is most inappropriate now. There is an intense need for you to trust your security within the world, and each and every one of you has a purpose. By accepting that purpose, by accepting who you are, by accepting what you understand and know, you then free yourselves from certain laws that govern density of being, allowing you to enjoy other laws that govern more subtle aspects of who you are. We see you as glorious. We acknowledge your beauty, as beauteous you are. You have a special place in time. You are approaching a period of criticality of consciousness, which is achieving what has not been achieved before. You are attaining understanding of a completeness and true nature of being, while being subject to dense vibrations and laws, and being able to transform these laws while being able to accept consciousness at levels that have not previously been attained.

You have a word, alchemy, which demonstrates most accurately what you are activating within yourselves now. It is not the physical alchemy that you are connecting or exploring. It is the spiritual, cosmic alchemy that can allow you to transcend the density of your reality to explore other co-operative consciousnesses within the framework of the universe. You are becoming the magician, but you are experiencing this magic at a level never before attained. You are regarded as being special by, in your terms, making the sacrifice to leave the level of spirit, to forget who you are, to exercise the plausibility of creating a time, an alchemical time, within a density of being that has never been present before, and which is being facilitated by those other beings who chose to remain in less dense forms of consciousness, but who still co-operate and assist where necessary.

So we smile as we observe your achievement. We acknowledge your progression and we make clear within the brotherhood and sisterhood of being, within the mother-father aspect of all that is, with absoluteness, that you are fast approaching a time when we will be as one, within one, throughout oneness, and the timelessness of being. Try to diminish the darkness of thought from our objective observations and allow yourselves to bathe in the constellation of the Milky Way, allowing each star to tickle and vibrate against your skin, allowing you to feel and experience your contact with us through the constellations.

SIX

The True Essence of Ascension

Visualise a circle of light. Place two free-standing triangles, facing each other, at opposite ends of the circle, like a mirror image. Allow them to lean in towards each other, so that their apexes touch. This is the central point of the circle. Allow the beam of light that emanates from the circle to become an intense beam of light as it comes from with the earth and is projected upwards. The point at the top becomes a prism. The white diffused light emanating from the circle itself becomes a deep indigo blue as it ascends and permeates the heavens.

Place your mind within the circle, and allow your mind to free-float within the environment as it is contained within the two triangles. Sense, if you can, a feeling of lightness and of buoyancy. This is time to feel an experiential attachment to tangible realities within the spiritual, emotional condition.

We announce ourselves as a spiritual consciousness to bring a perspective to the cosmic weight that has been created within this environment. This allows you to more gently identify and touch, through your sensory capabilities and experience, your own individual wisdom with the essence of the objective reality that is being projected to you as you tap into the vibration of these words.

Try and enjoy the feeling that the mind experiences within this new environment. The structure which you visualise contains you more within your physical reality, yet at the same time extends the parameters of your receptivity. Feel yourself connecting at the level of your heart. Draw the energy from these words at the level of their heart vibration. Draw as much as you feel you need. There is a limitless reservoir from which to take what is rightfully yours, knowing that we are all part of the same, aspiring to an absolute constant from which we fundamentally emanate.

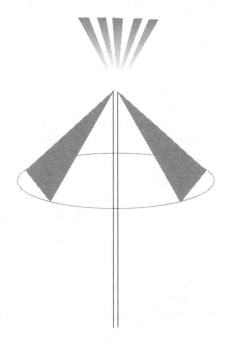

Attach a golden thread from your crown and feel it joining the centre of the circle at a point above the violet ray, bringing the

*conscious and unconscious together as one with the spiritual and
the cosmic. Allow complete integration at all levels within your
reality, as you understand it.*

We wish to talk about the specialness of this time, as you
are emotionally evolving through time, putting great effort
and energy into raising your awareness into dimensions of
which you have no conscious knowledge. We come in
response to validate who you are; to give you confirmation
of what you are achieving.

We are working simultaneously with your mind and heart
in a way that is normally separated as far as communication
is conveyed to you, understanding that you have reached a
point of development where it is no longer sufficient for you
to experience the reality of spirit on its own. There is now a
need, not to justify, but to allow the mind to explore its
untouched aspect, giving it the opportunity to sense the areas
in which it needs to develop.

You have reached a point in time when the density of your
feelings is bringing you to a level of understanding where
you find your reality encroaching on the intolerable, where
life appears to be more about understanding suffering than
appreciating the virtues of love, joy and contentment. As
with all density, as you reach higher, as you confirm who
you are within each reality as you experience it, there is a
need for your density of being to decrease, to allow the
upward momentum to continue. It is essential, therefore,
that you believe what you experience, or what you know, at
each level as you experience it, so that you can trust the
experience and absorb and live the understanding. It makes
it easier and causes less friction if you can accept who you
are at each stage, at each rung of the ladder.

You are ascending. Have no doubt. You are all at various

stages of ascension. This word seems to send out a clarion call to many among you, to whom ascension is much talked about as a means of leaving the Earth. Observe it, please, more as a means of achieving new consciousness states of being rather than any sense of displacement to another physical reality. We do not rule out the possibility of leaving the Earth's environment. Understand that there are those who are chosen to be removed in this way owing to who they are, rather than what they have done or achieved. You are largely still part of the spiritual-emotional cycle of evolution. It is to this that you have committed yourselves and it is to this end that you all seek fulfilment. It is the divine source of who you are that will maintain your balance within this progression to allow you to achieve ultimately that which you sacrificed first to take on dense form. Being as you are, in dense form, you only see or are aware of that which you can perceive within this density of being. The communication that is being made manifest within this space is endeavouring to create awareness of those unseen realities, as they are, with a sense of objectivity that often may seem harsh.

Visualise, for a moment, a wooden cross in the centre of your circle of light. It is representative of the one who sacrificed himself. The sacrifice is symbolic. What in actual fact the sacrificed was is consciousness itself. The consciousness of Christ-ing that, through the physical offering, became a physical energy-force within itself. It was allowed to permeate the Earth through the physical acts of bleeding, sweating, passing on physical moisture and liquid into the earth. The offering was with supreme intent so that, when the timing was right, this energy could be evoked again to stimulate those who understand. To become aware. To re-awaken and see what needs to be seen. You are now undergoing a process where you are coming into contact with your own Christ-ing. It is part of a global stimulus to which many are rising, from the apathy of the ego-centred being, to become more aware of the offering that was made in ancient time. The pressure that you experience is almost a knock-on effect from the pressure that was created at the time of the offering.

You are both evolving and involving at the same time while progressing through time and allowing your own wisdom to speak more clearly. You are also acquiring innocence to allow yourselves to see that which is. This is important as, within your reality, there are many illusions that are now losing their influence and their importance, and it is necessary for you to see your reality as it is for you, as this does not naturally correspond anymore to the reality that surrounds you. It is important that you enjoy and accept your own strength and allow this to evoke within you your creativity, your resourcefulness and your love. Your love for Self. Once that love is accepted and recognised, you can then recognise that love in others to whom the same process has been given. So the sense of recognition you have with those you see in the street is all that is needed. No words need to be communicated. You understand. You see those who are as you are, and know you are not alone.

Ascension

As you ascend towards your spiritual destiny you bring with you those with whom you have had contact, for the seeds you have sown within the minds of those who doubt will take root. It is spring, fast approaching summer, giving these seeds the opportunity to come into being. You will see and experience this over the next few years, whereby who you are, and those you have come into contact with, will become more vibrant and more visible within your own extended consciousness. Allow yourselves now the time to look back and reflect on those you have had contact with, and enjoy the satisfaction of seeing and recognising the productivity of the seeds you have sown in others. This is the reward. This is why you are here. This is all that needs to be achieved.

As you ascend the spiritual vibration, it is not so much that you suffer more, but you are more acutely aware of your own limitations as dense beings. What you experience, therefore, is a fear of your own limitations, of your own inadequacy, of how little you feel you can do to resolve the situation. This human feeling is merely an outward reflection of your restricted movement. Understand that fundamentally what you are doing is observing. So the experience of life itself can be transported into consciousness itself in its eternal and unified state in order to bring about a revolution of understanding within the subtle realms of existence; to bring about a greater cohesion of understanding of the evolving human condition within the emotional spiritual reality, thereby alerting those who assist to co-operate more productively.

You are glorious. Why do you fear that which you are? You are loving. Why do you feel the need to destroy that which you have difficulty in accepting within yourselves? You are peace-makers. Why do you feel the need to create tension and friction where it does not exist? You create obstacles for yourselves, so you can experience the path to enlightenment. The friction, the obstacles, are part of the experience. It is a part of the testing you create for yourselves to understand the value of who you are. There is a need for you to encounter difficulty, for you to understand that difficulty itself is not an issue, it is merely effort made manifest to make your progress visible. It is not a natural state of being. It is merely a mental projection of what you are endeavouring to create within your reality, making it more tangible.

Do understand, however, that you are now approaching a time when an awareness of the suffering caused by these manifestations of difficulty are no longer appropriate. Being alert and trusting, but more importantly, accepting the very nature of your being and what is communicated intuitively within you, will alert you to the direct root, to your own source-Self. The only quest in life is to be. There is nothing else. That is all. No more, no less. Nothing else has to be achieved. There is nothing else to reach for. There is no effort. In being, there is visibility of Self. In being, there is purpose. By being, there is love present. By being, you enjoy eternal peace.

Now visualise a golden ring above the centre of your circle of light, about six feet (2m) in diameter. See it spinning. It is creating a vacuum which is drawing you up, allowing your mind to be drawn up through the ring into another reality. Once you enter into this reality be within it. If you see images enjoy them. If you feel something allow yourself to absorb the experience. You are being drawn into an area of consciousness individual to you as you experience it. It is part of the eternal sun which energises matter into being, and it is this state which generates your own higher consciousness.

Look on this reality as such, as distinctly personal to you, but understand that for everyone who has been drawn into this reality, it is common to all. Try to comprehend the fluidity, the sense of independence of who you are. So that when you revert back into your dense self you bring an essence of what this means, and this bubble can transmit itself to each cellular part of your being. Now draw yourself back through the golden ring, and allow your mind to be where it was before, as the golden ring is dissolved.

As the knots of unconsciousness are untied within your state of being, understand that you will come to know the pure erotic state of being that is possible within the denseness of your body; that the time will come when you will no longer have amnesia on entering the physical state; that you will have reached a time of supreme power and will bring with you pure consciousness into active conscious vibrancy. This is the penultimate journey, for when this happens you will have reached the stage when the shell of the physical body will finally be discarded as you transmute into the new race, into the new being of consciousness that will stand on the Earth as pure consciousness itself. It is at that point in time that you will be released. Indeed, the Earth will release you from its attachment, allowing you to leave the environment of the solar system as you know it, to move to a different aspect within your galaxy to find and connect with a more permanent home. This will allow the Earth the opportunity to transmute itself into pure consciousness, knowing that its solar system will have enjoyed its cycle to the full; allowing it to be as energetic as it needs to be. That influence can then be better transmitted to other aspects within the physical framework of the universe, so that it can enlighten those who, at that time, may be in need.

There are those of you within the emotional-spiritual condition who are releasing yourselves now in preparation for this time, to be able to assist those who will need aiding in this transmutation. This will be the final epoch within your historical evolution as emotional beings. You are bound and supported so very closely within the framework of the Earth that the pathways between the different spiritual realities are very clear and are more tangible than they have ever been. Accept your Christ-ing. Accept the essence of what you represent. The cross is not a symbol of sacrifice. It is the arm outstretched as the ultimate gesture of acceptance which is achieved through surrender, not with any sense of dejection but with a sense of elation. To be able to recognise that you have reached a time when you can let go of dependence, you can then begin to spiral out of your reality and have the ability to appreciate the more subtle realities as they work with you.

The passing of the millennium will see great deterioration within the political economic structure that you have in western society. This deterioration is going to be used by those in less privileged circumstances as a means to create even greater disharmony while endeavouring to create another illusory structure as a power base for themselves. This will never be achieved. It will create some emotional distress within the civilised world, and there will be those who will feel lost and who will panic as the structure on to which they have projected their dependency is no longer present. We say this merely to illustrate the importance of you being able to love your own strength and to use this widely to create stability within your own personal environment, allowing you to bend in the wind knowing that the more flexible you are, the easier it will be for you to return to your natural state once the wind dies away.

There is much talk of war at a global level. Please look at your world. You already have war at a global level but in a way that you have not previously experienced. Different aspects within society are at odds with themselves. Look at the belief structures involved with those who are in dispute. They are largely very dense and very rigid. It is those people who contain within themselves the freedom not to believe, not to live their lives through any sense of containment, but who can allow themselves to move freely at the mental level, who are best adapted to change and who respond more positively than those who are kept within the belief structures that we speak about. The friction will remain until there is realisation of the fruitlessness of the exercise. There is no such thing as the victor. There is no such thing as the freedom fighter. Once the freedom fighter has attained power, then comes yet another belief structure and, in time, that structure too will need dissolving.

It is only the individual who has an awareness of the totality of his or her own being, who can achieve stability. It is this revolution within the spirit-mind that will have lasting effect within your state of being. Understand that you will resonate, you will connect, and you will create a reality for yourselves that will call like minds and like hearts around the world, creating a very strong, yet flexible, communication network which will fuse as one and will be indestructible.

This is the reality within which you are currently working. This is what you are creating. Observe it. See it. The darker denser realities of which we speak need not be part of your reality unless you choose them to be so. You will, however, experience some of the after-shocks as they come your way, and those of you who create this very strong belt of consciousness around the Earth, will decide at various points in time to offer yourselves, if you like, in sacrifice, to create explosions of awareness, in particular circumstances that can diffuse this friction. But also understand that such is the measure of your maturity that this can be allowed.

Energetic Implants

The Christ-consciousness emanates from where it was created in the Middle East, and the vibration within this area is actually at its strongest, which is why you have there one of the most tense areas of friction within the Earth. Understand also that there are energetic implants surrounding this whole area which are magnifying the essence of what this Christ-ing represents, so that it may be conveyed to the rest of the world and indeed transmitted to those other forms of intelligence and consciousness who are at work in co-operation with who we are.

There are secrets within the northern aspects of Egypt that will be revealed towards the end of the first decade in the new millennium. These secrets will be given to some who can use the divine power emanating from this area of the Middle East in a way that can create a quantum leap in consciousness of the world mind. Within the ancient land of Persia, as it existed, there is also another energetic implant. There are going to be those beings who will come from outside the Earth and will reveal this energy implant. They will use this to reflect onto the earth the representation of what is contained within it. This will allow those who can see and use that, to facilitate it in a practical way around the world, as the levels of that communication into which technology will have vaulted, at that point in time, will allow the effectiveness of this revelation to be immediate and conclusive.

There is another energetic implant in the eastern aspect of the Mediterranean. This aspect is going to have an effect on the physical structure of the Earth itself as it communicates directly with certain mineral compositions within it, alerting the Earth to a different change in its own magnetic quality as it will be drawn into a slightly different position within the solar system. This is being worked on directly at this present time.

These are the major energetic implants that will effect your physical-emotional reality. We speak of them mainly to activate awareness of your own divinity in relation to the Christ-consciousness itself. It is not practical at this time to create awareness of other happenings that might be possible within your Earth, as it may cloud how you view your future. We illustrate mainly to enlighten, not to discourage or dismay, and within this you must accept that there is a limit to what can actually be voiced.

We can say that the combination of all these areas of magnetism will intensify your experience of the Earth plane, allowing those of you who have reached a sufficient vibration to be free of its influence. But those who are still contained within it will experience a strong degree of emotional disturbance. In many ways you are experiencing the disturbance already yourselves so that you may be in a better position to be able to assist and help those who seek aid.

Believe in who you are. Believe in the choices that you have made. Accept the workings of the absolute. Accept the systems from all levels as they are offered. Merely allow yourselves to be available and alert, and respond as instinctively as you feel is appropriate. You carry within you a consciousness that comes not of the Earth. This is often what you call wisdom. Allow this to work with you. Accept what you know. Accept this understanding that often is beyond words. It is becoming more tangible. Allow yourselves to respond instinctively without thought.

You are reaching a point in time when you will not be able to justify your actions, but it is this instinctive part of who you are that is going to alert you to appropriate action.

You are becoming like the fireball – a golden energetic vehicle – that flies around the Earth creating a wind which people experience. This golden wind will create friction in the minds and hearts of others, allowing them to experience what you represent, creating a sense of comfortableness within spiritual union, as you float on the river of truth, gently and purposefully; as you soak up the sun which is allowing you to regenerate and grow in honesty and openness, accessible and vibrant.

Know this. Know who you are. Accept your loving being, and enjoy the realities as you experience them. They will become increasingly more precious as you ascend. The velocity that you acquire will take you outside time itself as you experience the unity and oneness of all.

SEVEN

The Changing Face of Earth

Visualise yourself, if you will, sitting in a circle with the floor as molten gold. Imagine a vortex being created in the centre of the circle, extending so that it encompasses the whole circle itself, as though you are suspended above a golden vortex of energy penetrating the earth itself. Imagine, above your head, a transparent crystal canopy creating a mirror image, and allow another vortex to create itself in the centre of the circle above your head. Allow it to extend outwards so that it embraces the whole circle, extending upwards into infinity. Know that you are now suspended in time in an energetic vacuum, achieving a sense of balance between the density of your reality and the likeness of our presence, freeing you from any energetic interference that might impede into your space. Allow your mind to experience itself as free-floating, allowing it the unconscious ability to attune itself with a more Earthly frequency, or with a higher frequency, to maintain its balance within this form of communication.

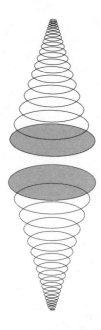

We wish to make you aware of the motion within the planets themselves contained within your solar system; to enable you to understand that quite apart from the dissolution of the dense structure that you have within your society, you also experience the evolution of your own planetary system. Know that each of these planets in turn, like the Earth, needs, by virtue of their being, to expand themselves within their own framework of consciousness which exists for them; that they themselves are alert to the change with all the various consciousness forms that exist within the solar system and are also altering their own concentration of being, of matter and composition.

Your scientists are currently aware of a progressive and somewhat erratic force emanating from your sun in as much as it is not consistently emitting impulses at the same rate as those which have been previously observed. It is now combusting at a faster rate, giving off more energy, more heat, more light, more radioactivity – raw, vital components of energy that are rebounding off all the planets within your system. This activates all energetic structure within your solar system, breaking down and dissolving the more unstable minerals and organic compounds within each planet in turn, so that they themselves are undergoing a distinct change in constitutional content.

As a result, some of these planets are emitting gases which were stored within them. Some of the substances are becoming more liquid, more molten, and some of the large densities of material are being broken down to their component parts, thereby releasing the latent energy stored within them, creating a greater force-field of activity within the solar system itself. In practical terms, it would not be entirely inaccurate to say that your environment is becoming more radioactive. It is being destabilised at a level that is only minutely measurable, but it is present nevertheless. Know that this accumulation of minute instability will eventually acquire a critical density which will bring about a dissipation, causing a complete change within the energy structure of your solar system itself, which will in turn have major ramifications within your galaxy.

In simplistic terms, it is easier for us to say that what is happening in respect to your planetary system is happening to you, to your minds, to the consciousness that you contain within yourselves. But as the increase in activity within the solar system progresses, you – as dense, energetic beings – will begin to sense and feel the pressure that is exerted on your beings by these physical changes. It is with our co-operation that you can bring yourselves into balance, to re-stabilise yourselves by allowing us to create force-fields that you can tap into and draw into your energetic beings to maintain this stability. Remember that you are firmly established within an energetic net of being which allows you to draw on this resource.

At the moment, the force-field that is exerted by your solar planetary system and the magnetic forces that are contained within this system imply that this change, for the moment, will be contained within your system. We say this to illustrate the need for you to be able to hasten your own development to maturity, to allow you to stand on the outside of your solar system. We say this to give a perspective to what we have said previously, and to bring a more immediate sense of practicality for your need to attain this level of maturity. It is this which is most important to achieve over the next 50 years, and for the majority of the beings here, for this to be completed within the next 20 to 25 years – and this is possible.

So, we are illustrating in another way the need for you to attain this objectivity that we speak of, to allow your minds, to allow your soul-beings to stand outside the volatile nature of the change, the physical change, that is happening within the encapsulation of your solar system.

This effect will hasten the destabilisation of the Earth's environment, allowing some of the situations that we have already touched upon to come into being. This new magnetic force, or pull, will create new land masses, allowing the ones that are now defunct to be crumpled up and submerged as they no longer have practical value. Your Earth can no longer sustain life at the level that it needs to, so the toxicities can then be reabsorbed, transformed and reused in other ways.

Transition Time

As more gases are released within the solar system, different atmospheric conditions will prevail which will start to interfere with your ionosphere, allowing the ionic charge to become more vibrant, creating a denser, moister atmosphere within the Earth's environment itself. As a result, the structure of your lungs needs to change in order to be able to respire within a greater density of air which holds within it, for simplicity's sake, aqueous solution. Therefore, a lot of the moisture that you bring into your body will come through means of respiration, and the need for you to drink to obtain moisture will decrease. However, it does mean that the quality of your atmosphere needs to be clean. It also means that because of the density of the air, any heavy particles that are emitted into the atmosphere will actually be earthed and absorbed.

During this transition time, before the emitting of pollution into the atmosphere, in order for your lungs to acquire the shape, form and size that they need to, there will be a need for your race to be underground, to be under the oceans, and to re-collect yourselves and re-establish a habitat that you once enjoyed in times that are long forgotten. You will recapture this habitat and re-cultivate intuitively. Indeed, we would like to suggest that there are consciousness forms contained within the Earth with whom you have lost contact, who can guide you to understand what you need to know to facilitate this progress. In preparation for going underground and under the sea, you will reach an awareness that will enable you to connect with the different consciousnesses that you are not connecting with at the moment. You will see them. It is that simple. It is that clear.

You may be wondering when, in your time-frame, you will be going underground and under the ocean. Let us say that it will be out of your time. It will be a little beyond your time, but not too far. The beams of light and also the space-ships that you cannot see at the moment will help you make this move underground. There are extenuating circum-stances that are largely subject to – it is difficult for us to describe – political circumstances, even though the word political in this time will be very different to what you know now, which will facilitate this change. The word political is perhaps most inappropriate and we use it only in the context of group motivating force. But group motivating force, as we understand this to be in this time, will be contained within groups of individuals with intuitive understanding of need. These individuals will be able to motivate other groups of individuals, so there will be, in many respects, a chain reaction. We do not suggest that everyone will move in this way. Indeed it is not required that everyone moves in this way.

Again, it is difficult to describe, but there will be very advanced spiritual beings who will act as caretakers for groups of people. There will not be any sense of aban-donment of those who feel they cannot make that journey and who wish to remain above ground. Indeed it is important that life above ground is maintained, as the psychological balance within the density of your beings needs to be still complete in its essence. It is also essential for the experience to be conveyed to bring about even more complementary understanding of the versatility and multi-dimensional nature of your being.

Greater stimulation will be given to the hypothalamus and the optic nerve, to enable you to adapt to this change as the body's metabolism will need to change in relation to this new environment as there will no longer be the opportunity for the body to aerobically expire at the level that it used to, so certain functions within the body need to be speeded up and others need to become totally dormant. You will lose the need to be physically strong, and in turn will become more dextrous and flexible within your movement. The food that is provided within the Earth itself will, at this time, match the need of the body. The food that will be provided will be light, with large contents of carbohydrate and vitamins and vegetable protein. There will no longer be a need for you to assimilate the heavier, richer foods that you currently enjoy. Also your ability to sustain energy will be increased, consequently the need to physically consume food will decrease.

It is important, therefore, to re-emphasise what we have said in relation to the radiation that you create on your planet. This needs to be sufficiently curtailed for at that point in time as you endeavour to live under the ground and under the sea, this highly unstable matter will begin to break free of its containment. You are liable to then be subjected to those specific vibrations within your solar atmosphere that you are endeavouring to be immune from. Energy may have to be employed to remove this radioactive waste, as you term it, and place it within the context of the environment that you will not be using at that particular time – which will largely be above ground. What you are entering into at the moment is a process of moving it around. You cannot hide it. It will not go away.

As we understand it, all will be done so that intolerable levels are not produced and stored, but we do feel that we need to alert you to the situation as a whole, as we believe it exists. We say: tell your friends, so they know too. Radioactive energy is very much a part of all energetic force within the universe. It is a natural force, and where it occurs seemingly at random within your earth, it is there for a purpose. There are other beings within the universe who can use this energy wisely in its natural state, and draw on it directly as a means of power. Part of your evolution allows you to understand the need to tap into this limitless source of power, but the crude manner in which you are approaching this, has proved, without a doubt, that the current method is not productive. Within your own economic structure it is not productive. To believe it is, is an illusion. A cycle has been started which your political structure is trying to justify, but without success.

As your science of astronomy progresses and becomes more technologically evolved, those who work within that science will be able to see and monitor the emanations coming from the various planets, and will observe among most of the planets the development of rings. These rings will vary from being molecularly thin, to creating a complete opaque covering around the planets themselves, almost like a dust that is held in suspension. As this occurs, it means that those beings who work in co-operation with you, who travel in vessels of transportation, will become more visible. This visibility is necessary in order to penetrate through the new density that is being created within your solar reality.

It is interesting perhaps to comment that, at the point in time when you can see and observe will be the time when you will go underground and under the oceans. That will enable those who work in co-operation to clear and prepare the surface for rehabilitation. As you re-emerge once more, it is then that there will be total co-operation and conscious acknowledgement of the complementary nature of being. You will have reached that point when you can accept and work alongside those, figuratively speaking, whom many of you now distrust.

But this is progress. This is a very real form of evolution of the mind and of your understanding, and the time that we speak of is very much in your future. As the density within your solar reality increases, it will reach a new point of criticality which, again, will create another dispersion or dissipation, bringing about a more complete and radical change. It is at this point that you, as we have said previously, will begin to glow, change and leave your dense form. You will still maintain shape, but will become energy matter. It is at this point that you yourselves will be able to blend with radioactivity as we understand it, and use that as an energy force for transmigration, enabling you to be within whatever reality is attracting you at that time.

We speak of transmigration not as a concept, but as a reality. It is important for you to grasp this reality as you will come to experience it within the psycho-emotional state as you understand it at this present time. It is literally transferring consciousness to another place, perhaps within another form, so that in your psycho-emotional state, as you pass close to the planets, and as you rest on the planets themselves, it will be possible – when you leave this Earth – to allow your mind and your consciousness to actually enjoy a reality in another time-space while still being part of the psycho-spiritual cycle. Indeed you will reach the stage when you will be able to give yourselves away to this process voluntarily as you realise that this work has been completed within the Earth environment, and to invite cosmic stickiness the opportunity to transport you to another time-place whilst bringing with you, in full, the consciousness that you represented while being in the Earth environment. In your sleep state you are already experiencing the possibilities of these journeys as they make themselves known to you.

New Forms of Healing

When you experience the raw energy that is involved in these journeys, it evokes what you call nightmares, as we observe them, where what you are experiencing in abstract form in your sleep proves to be so disturbing on the psycho-emotional state that you have some difficulty maintaining the process. But understand that your mind is very alert to your physical needs. It draws you back at the moment of any uncomfortableness that may take you to a level beyond your tolerability. So there is a mechanism in place to stop you enduring more than you can. In the dream state you are also being taught about the evolution of your physical bodies, to allow you to be more alert about what you need in order to enhance its vitality. This is one of the reasons why there is a great embrace towards what you call complementary medicine. As you understand more and more the energetic nature of your being, you understand – you don't know – but you do understand that you can maintain your vitality through contact with other energetic forms of regeneration. There are some who embrace this with such totality that they tend to forget, or ignore, the possibilities of what science can offer.

While you are partaking of the process of evolution, understand that you do still need to partake of all. Your complementary arts are actually a reflection of your medical applications; they are growing at relatively the same rate and represent in evolutionary terms much the same scale or ratio. There is balance, and it will be brought to a clearer focus of union, as indeed science and esoteric awareness are beginning to understand and acknowledge their Selves.

You are also, in your dream state, being focused or integrated more firmly with time itself in your terms. The ability to avoid any situation is becoming less prominent and more and more you will be drawn to that which you need to understand and face. This form of operation is increasing with great speed which may, perhaps, allow you to understand the pain and the suffering within your reality as well as its polarised opposite – the love and the joy.

As you are working with much speed, it is time now for you to resolve your relationships at all levels, in all time-spaces, with whatever moment is freely available so, in your terms, your sleep state is becoming more active, and your dreams are becoming more intense as you work to resolve these relationships. It means that you have fewer periods of tranquillity and waking refreshed. As you do resolve these relationships, you will experience larger periods of peace and quietude.

To expand on this, let us explain that you choose a spiritual family in which to enjoy the psycho-spiritual cycle. To reach that point of divinity which you first lost when you took on a physical body, you need to reach an agreement within the contract you have undertaken to explore under-standing through your emotional context. As you reach this agreement with each spiritual individual with whom it was first made, you then free yourselves of this contract within your psycho-emotional condition, enabling you to work purely at the level of spirit and in service.

As you grow in awareness of the absolute and understand how you can work more closely, more immediately with it, this releases you into a form of consciousness beyond which the DNA cannot contain you further. It is difficult for us to describe in your words. We talked earlier about there being, in your terms, a limit of consciousness memory that the DNA could contain within it, and indeed change into. It is at the point of true realisation, where knowing, understanding and being are fused as one, that you become liberated.

You may wonder how your spiritual healing will develop during this process. Let us say that this term will be redundant. The term as you use it now is becoming a rather inaccurate description of what you do. You will reach the stage where your fingers become convectors of heat, of light and of sound – almost within the context of laser technology as you have embraced it presently. It will be more direct in terms of removing dense, physical disharmony, particularly in relation to cancer.

But do understand that there will be a great deal of focus in actually changing the memory within the person being treated, thereby removing at first hand the potential for disease itself. So you become resonating magnets emitting very strong force-fields which people will come to bathe within to alert themselves, or release themselves from force-fields that are, for them, largely inappropriate. The healing of dense physical disharmony is largely going to be the removal of the physical disease after having resolved the spiritual-psychological disharmony that created the manifestation of the disease or the disharmony in the first place.

You will reach the point where the healer, as you understand it, is redundant as energetic places of com-munion will offer people the opportunity to regenerate themselves. Medicine, in your terminology, will also be largely redundant as most of your work will be focused in the area of well-being, rather than curing, and maintaining the level of well-being will have a greater influence, a greater impact, within your society. This will take place, in your time, in 150 years.

Never before have you been so active within so many dimensions within the instant, and this is a reflection on you, and how you have successfully developed through time. As a result, there is a great need for you to accomplish your learning, in order to assist all those in your dimension, to enable them to complete what needs to be done. We hope this gives some clarity to the separation we talked of earlier. So in simplistic terms, there is greater need for soul essences to be within the spiritual reality than the physical reality, as there are more soul essences needed in co-operation to help each individual in turn.

Please keep in context what has been said. Try and contain it within the level of understanding rather than knowledge. Allow it to grow there, as it will alert you more at that level to your own responsibilities, than it will at the level of knowledge.

Now it is time to bring you back to your visualisation. Focus once more on the energy vortex above your head and allow it to telescope into a pure violet crystal canopy. Feel the liquid gold firming beneath you and filling up the space beneath your feet, so that once more you are buoyant above the golden, molten mass. Allow the image gradually to dissolve as you bring yourself now back to your own reality.

EIGHT

Your Relationship with Time

Visualise a silver sphere in the centre of a circle. Imagine it is cut into eight pieces, and allow it to open like a flower. Imagine a little disc rising from it like a platform, so it is suspended approximately six inches (5 cm) above the sphere itself. Place your mind on this elevated disc. Allow the disc to now descend into the middle of the silver sphere, which is open. Sense the difference between where you have placed your mind and your physical body.

We wish to now talk about your psychology, and time. The relationship that your mind has with time. You have an awareness of the conscious and the unconscious. You are aware of hidden feelings, of sensations, of senses, of a knowing that goes beyond comprehensive understanding, which cannot be justified within rational sensibility. You have feelings, and you have feelings that go beyond the emotional level; that go into the area of the inexplicable, where the point of origin, the point of stimulus of these

feelings, is unknown. And it is these unknown impulses that, because you cannot justify them, you have habitually tended to ignore. As a result, you have tended to live your lives within the illusions of the structures you have created for yourselves. Now is the time to adjust and feel, in your terms, where the impulses are coming from; to develop a sense of knowing, of what these impulses are, and what their presence means – and to place these within the clairvoyant and psychic content, as you understand them, within the format of communication.

What do you like to feel? You all like to feel love. You all like to feel pleasure, sensuality, degrees of light and shade, colour and sound. These are all within the spectrum of your capability of feeling. Within your emotional context there is fear, joy, pain, pleasure, anxiety, uncertainty. In many ways all of these things are part of the one. Within the emotional, feeling, psychological make-up of your being, they are, in our terms, part of the same thing. So when we talk of emotions they include the full gamut of experience of what we have described. Feelings mainly pertain to everything outside of this, and are not to be confused, in this context, with sensory pleasure or sensory perception within the energetic nervous perspective of your physical selves. Psychology, as we understand it, is to do with perception of your reality, behavioural patterns and motivating qualities.

Time, as we understand it, is a form of continuum. Time is a drawing through experience, creating a friction that allows you to be alert and experience the instance. It is a vehicle that draws you through understanding, but a vehicle without motion or momentum, a plane within reality. Within this plane it allows you to plot experiences, giving them fixed co-ordinates so that when you wish to return to them, to recreate them, to remember them, it is possible to connect with them easily. This is true for all of you.

Within your density of being, you approach time within a linear form of structure that is given certain values, and it is to these values that you attach experience. Everything, therefore, is compartmentalised and has its own place. And within time, within this realm of existence, you have reached a point, a co-ordinate, where your psychology is changing and being changed; where your make-up, your composition, is being reorganised in a different manner. You have reached a point where your psychology, as it has been, is no longer relevant. It has no function but to catapult you into your future. What does this mean in your terms? We have talked of your need to be dependent. We have talked of you expressing yourselves, of relating to other individuals within your plane of existence, within the framework of love, and within the framework of organic composition as you are connected to the Earth and to the universe.

Living Your Truth

We have also shown how you are only perceptive to that which you can perceive. This would suggest that you are approaching a time now when you are going to be receptive to that which you cannot perceive. If you do not perceive something, how do you then bring yourselves to a point where you can? By allowing yourselves to experience and develop a sense of trust within yourselves; by allowing those subtle inner feelings a greater validity than they have had previously. As these feelings become more consistent and seem to expand and radiate, they will naturally magnetise others towards you with greater impact.

Within your psychic faculty of developing your third eye – of expanding your sight within previously unseen realities – is a reality now which you are all being brought towards. But there is a difference between this and, as you understand it, psychic development, as what you are now beginning to develop for yourselves is a sense of knowing. This is outside any sense of rational learning. It is outside the area of intuition. You do not sense it. You do not feel it. You do not experience it, but you know it. It is there. It is resonant. It is an object that is solid in its insubstantial being.

What does this mean therefore? It means that you are being brought to a stage when the mask you hide behind as a personality begins to slip, and it is no longer possible for you to communicate behind any guise or front. This will cause you to be totally honest, open and available. It means your ability to deceive will be diminished. This is largely to do with you acquiring maturity through time.

As you understand that deception has no validity as it

perpetuates the illusion; that as the illusion itself is crumbling and beginning to dissolve, there is no way in which you can now perpetuate its existence. For some, this will provide them with a sense of relief, for others it is going to evoke fear as they will have to be who they are; they will have to be honest with themselves and true to their expression. If you like, your history, your karma, that which you have experienced outside of your current time-space is reaching a point of critical density, which can no longer be contained within your psychological spiritual make-up as it is presently.

If this is the motivating force of your learning process, then this means that you can no longer draw on your karma without a greater or more complete understanding of the whole, as it, by virtue of its very being, is in many ways becoming unstable within itself. Therefore, there is a need for you to sever your connection with it. Or rather, in this space-time, allow ,yourselves to appreciate your greater whole.

So the devices that you now employ to deceive yourselves will become like knife-wounds in the heart. You will not be able to tolerate them. Those in your society who are waking up will no longer be able to tolerate this. It is as though somebody has peeled away the layer of your skin leaving you totally vulnerable, so that if anybody intrudes or touches you it causes immense discomfort. There is therefore a need for you to be quite clear about who you are and what you express, so that those who might ordinarily intrude upon or contact your creative space will be able to read and see quite clearly your intent and, most importantly, know and understand what is meant.

The healing known as the healing of the archetypes is, in many ways, one of your illusions as the archetype itself is an illusion. There is no such thing as an archetype. You are not defined in such contained terms. You tend to do that for yourselves as a means of explanation and justification. You are not and never will be an archetype, one thing, a representation of – this is not possible. You are too complex and multi-faceted to be contained within this. It is a device used by some to explain and elucidate a particular hypothesis, giving individuals the opportunity to see, within another format, their representation.

In our terms, this representation is totally illusory and inaccurate in many ways, and for us holds no real value. But as used by those individuals who express it, it has limited effect. As you understand that, it is in itself limited. There is no need for this to be expressed within your healing reality. It is merely an aspect, a tiny aspect of who you are.

We wish to draw a mental picture of you living on a gigantic rubbish dump. You believe this rubbish dump is glorious and provides for all your needs. None of you are prepared to admit that it is rotten, that it stinks and actually needs to be cleared away. Then the rubbish dump actually reaches a point when its smell is so intense that it cannot be tolerated. The decomposition happening within it is actually making the rubbish dump itself unstable, and there is a possibility that parts of it may explode because it is so toxic. But you ignore it at your peril. It is necessary not for one of you but for all of you to own up to the fact that this is how it is. To own up to the truth of your experience, to be able to convey what is within it is of absolute importance. You can no longer couch what you say in a comfortable form of expression that eases truth into the reality of those around you.

Total Reality

The co-ordinates of your time clarify that you have reached a point when the human mind experiences total reality. In and out of consciousness you experience all the realities with which you are connected. You do not remember all, but you experience all. This co-ordinate, which you have now reached, has never been encountered before within your spiritual context. Your mind is being stimulated at so many different levels that, unless it responds to all the impulses that it receives, it will no longer be able to perpetuate itself within the spiritual-psychological condition. Therefore the need to be real and to express your realness is important, not only to yourselves as individuals but to you as a group within society, as a society within humanity.

It is difficult for us to describe, but if we say that each point in history has its own straight line to this co-ordinate that you call now, then there is a complete inter-relation of time in the now, and all experience of all things in all time-space is being brought into this co-ordinate. This co-ordinate embraces more than this instance, it embraces a cosmic level of being that encompasses many years.

We cannot define, in your terms, how long or how many years are contained within this co-ordinate. It is a developmental stage of your being, but every aspect of your being is beginning to reverberate in response to the criticality of your situation. If we trace the criticality through a quantum leap, we could look at it as a mirror image of the coming together of these points in time so that you, individually or as groups, are then propelled to various time-spaces within a continuum. As you pass through this critical time, it may not be appropriate for you to be within this time-space, and as you pass through this criticality you may be within another place within the physical framework of the universe. As you experience the coming together of all, you experience the total dissipation of all as it becomes scattered throughout the universe, and the various aspects of your consciousness then return to the origins of thought, the origins of conceptualisation from whence they first originated, going back to the one.

But within this context there are many different ones, understanding of course that all of these ones are part of the whole. It is difficult to conceptualise aspects of thought as having a point of origin, but collectively, as a group, this is what will happen. This is the ultimate meaning of transmigration. There are stages in between, sometimes. As every aspect of your conceptualisation returns to your point of origin, it is at that moment that you understand all within the context of consciousness, as you experience it.

So we are now at the point of how your consciousness originated in the very first instance: it was a coming together of a million different aspects of energetic being – pure, singular, energetic being. And as it came together, it acquired a form of source. This form of source is consciousness, a product of the mother-father principle. So when we talk of your consciousness, then talk of it travelling through the galaxy and acquiring a greater density as it enters your solar system, this may perhaps paint a greater picture of the enormity of what is contained within your consciousness. As each of your consciousnesses, as it pertains to each of you, is unique, it means that as you bring this consciousness into your physicality, it may allow you to appreciate the enormity of who you are, of what you naturally understand and know. Therefore, when we talk of you speaking from a point of knowing, it is because you have reached a level of maturity where you can bring this access to the greater consciousness into the open.

So we are not talking about clairvoyance or psychic awareness. We are talking about knowing what is. The terms that you use to describe awareness, progressive thought and development are, by themselves, now becoming inappropriate. Understand that when you communicate with other levels, it is not necessarily with the co-operation of other spiritual beings, or that you are listening to helpers or guides, though it is often easier to use these terms to complete a form of communication more quickly. It is actually that you are touching a like resonance outside of your own space-time. Whatever aspect of thought, of conceptualisation, you are engaged in, there is a sympathetic resonance to the source of that origin, and what you sense is the impulse coming from that source, as you communicate with it and with the being from it. You must now try to imagine yourselves as being a spot on a piece of graph-paper, and that time corresponds more to your position on this graph-paper than just a passage through experience.

Therefore, by being honest with yourselves, by being clear about who you are and your work within that reality, you can then communicate more freely, more easily, more comfortably, and this allows you to make available that which you already understand. So when you look into the future, you are actually looking into your very being. You have your future contained within you. What you have difficulty with, at the moment, is seeing beyond the point of criticality, and it is only over the last few years in your time that other thought-impulses have managed to be able to be attracted to each other to form a communication dynamic that can actually be transmitted into your space-time. And it is only in the last few years that those within your dimension have been sufficiently attuned to be able to receive in this manner.

The human communicator of these words has, in your terms, clairvoyant or psychic ability. In our terms, he is now speaking from his own point of view, his own point of truth. His truth has reached a level of flexibility, of liquidity, so that it can slowly be drawn or magnetised from him as a form of consciousness. We merely integrate our own thought-impulses with his as they extend into our reality, understanding that our reality, being in a different space-time continuum, is at a different point on your piece of graph-paper. But there is a sense of logic, in your terms, that this can be made possible, that it is mathematically feasible.

So when we talk of knowledge and of understanding, it is not always necessary to bring the understanding to the level of knowledge itself – which is stored information. It is far more appropriate to leave this understanding at the level where it is most active and pertinent. Until you can allow yourselves to be perceptive within the honesty of your beings, it is not appropriate to translate this understanding into more coherent rational terms. This is the greatest difficulty with which you struggle as you continually need to prove and to justify. You can accept who you are, with courage, and allow yourselves to live that which you be. But until that time you will continue to struggle, to rationalise what you already understand. As you become open and honest with yourselves, the truth will naturally flow. You will then know, and you will accept your knowing because you understand it.

What does this lead to? It leads to the release of behaviour patterns. You leave behind your habitual nature, allowing yourselves to continually be stimulated into newness, into fresh areas of activity, of conceptualised thought and feeling – and being able to accept comfortably whatever experience comes your way, knowing that you will be able to use it without anxiety. As you trust who you are and as you put fear, anxiety, habit and programmed behaviour behind you, this will allow you to draw towards yourselves creativity at a level never before experienced. It will allow you to bring into being, into practical being, a quality of life never before experienced.

Joy of the Mind

Within your co-ordinates you will be leaving behind effort. You will explore the joy of the mind and experience greater capacity. The leap that you will make will bring the percentage of the mind you use up to approximately 65% which, in your terms, is incomparable. The movement of your present co-ordinate to a new point is dependent on your own progression, and you can only proceed to a new co-ordinate if there is a group momentum that can propel you towards it. So, once again, you will never be in any situation you are not able to deal with. This is not how, it just is. It is neither arbitrary, nor is it accidental, and you are not being put through anything that you cannot tolerate or endure. So not only is there a need for you to dispel disharmony, there is a need for you to dispel any potential disharmony. You will come to this individually, and some of you will lead others in group situations to be able to experience the sense of freedom that we speak of. It will not be rushed. It will naturally evolve through your own efforts.

You can help those people who are just beginning their unfoldment and who are feeling this in their hearts, by showing them compassion. This will help bring their truth into being. Within compassion there is honesty of being. To show someone compassion is to show them an armchair of love in which they can recline. In many respects love is the motivating energy within the universe. By demonstrating this compassionately, you are showing others that it is acceptable to be compassionate, vulnerable and open. Open to give and to receive. It is simple, but it is fundamental. It will cause the illusions to crack, allowing each individual to see for themselves their real Self.

If all the information we are giving is already contained within you, you may wonder why it is necessary for us to send this information through this communicator and why we do not trigger that information direct within each of you?

We do it this way because we know that many of you have a need to justify and to have proof of who you are and where you are heading. You are drawn to reading this book and have triggered within you the momentum to lift you into a great awareness of your own unique consciousness being. There are ways and there are means. So we speak within a guise. We are facilitating a form of communication in the best way that we feel is possible. We see ourselves as evokers of intelligence so that you may see within yourselves that which is real and true for you. We cannot, nor wish to, bring you to a state where you see things in the purity of its own being. As you are all very different, compositionally, this is not possible. It also takes away from the very nature of your having a dense physical body and you need, through your own efforts, to reach those latent levels of understanding, of consciousness, that are secret to you. We cannot show to each and every one of you what is secret to you. We can make you aware of some aspect of how things are, and we speak in this way to confirm feelings that you have, but cannot voice.

You are all different. You are all experiencing this consciousness at more levels than you can possibly imagine. Through the projection of your mind into the energy structures that we create on your behalf, you are all absorbing aspects of this consciousness at the level you can accept. You then contain this energy within your energetic being. It is literally contained within your aura. As you pass by, and have contact with, other energetic levels of other individuals, this energy and this consciousness are naturally transmitted to them. It is not necessary to communicate in the manner that we are. The means at our disposal in this situation are limited and will always be so.

As you acquire a different tonality through accepting this vibratory communication you become, as you read this, more able through your vibratory make-up to hold this magnetised field that is descending, in many ways metaphorically, on to the Earth. Then everybody may be held within it and as you hold this field together, all this information is transmitted but it is not the specifics, it is the whole and it is the experience. It is the encounter of the whole which is of vital importance, not the aspects of which you read and feel within these words.

All of you are transmitters. You can absorb, hold and transmit an energy that is beyond your conscious comprehension, which activates others into consciousness. The activation is like the tiny seed rather than a garden of flowers, but without the seed, a single flower is not possible. You must see yourselves in these terms. It is as though, because of your need to justify, to prove, to see what you are doing, your desire – heartfelt, appreciated and acknowledged – is so far in front of you, that it evokes frustration in your inability, seemingly, to communicate what you feel must be. The frustration is of your own making.

We cannot reiterate enough that you are *already* communicating. You cannot communicate without receiving. You are receiving as you read this. Each of you, in your own right, have allowed yourselves in previous instances to receive.

What you receive, you naturally transmit. You must not try to emulate within limited terms that which another does. What you are experiencing is just a tiny fraction of what *is*. In your terms, the real world starts when you leave your home and move into society. That is when you activate others.

We endeavour to give you a greater appreciation of how you work and who you are. The greatest appreciation of this is knowing that you know. Allow yourselves to enjoy this sense. You are all keepers of your own wisdom. You are all guardians of your own uniqueness of being. You hold the keys. You will always know more than you can voice. Appreciate the knowing. Allow it to glow within you, and be satisfied, or allow yourselves to draw the peace and the warmth that are representative of that glow.

The reason we ask you to project your minds into the energy structures in the way that we do, at the start of each session, is to allow you the opportunity to connect with the origin of aspects of thought. It is not possible for you at this moment to bring this into conscious experience, but know that it is there and that it is part of the accumulation of all time experience in the now.

You are entering the golden age of your being. Gold for us is symbolic of your cosmic being, and the gold that we speak of is not represented within your dimension. Its vibration is beyond your experience. But know that those who work with you, who are lifting your minds to contact consciousness, are part of this golden being, and the magnetic field that contains the consciousness of this golden being is gently attracting you towards it.

The reason we call ourselves sun-consciousness is because of the golden emanation of our collective coming together. This is the predominant colour within which we pulsate. The visitations you have on your Earth, in ancient times often referred to as suns, are largely to do with this emanation.

Place your attention and mind once more in the silver orb. Allow the silver disc, with an aspect of your mind, to resurface and become suspended above this silver orb. Draw your mind back from it into yourself. See the suspended disc descend once more into the orb, and see the orb coming together as one, to be once more a solid entity. Allow this to gradually fade.

NINE

Your Future Passage Through Time and Space

Visualise, in the centre of a circle, a bed of vibrantly coloured flowers. Project all your senses towards these flowers; allow all these senses to dwell in and among them so that you smell, touch, taste, see and sense what they are about.

Allow a clear crystal pyramid to descend, covering both your senses and the flowers, so that all is contained within this pyramidal structure. Now observe this from your point of conceptual visualisation and regard the scene, so your senses are both within the pyramid and also looking through and into the clear crystal structure to what is within it.

Create a spiral of energy emanating from the apex of the pyramidal structure and ascending. The purpose of this spiral is to allow your senses to come into contact with consciousness itself through the vehicle of the spiral into the reality beyond matter. Keep contact with your senses and as this draws you up into it, into another dimension, evaluate the subtle change that occurs. It should draw you to a point, giving you the opportunity to regard this situation in objectivity, and see the reality of what is here, outside the illusion. Take a moment to explore this.

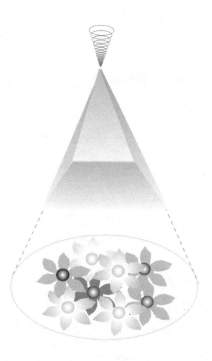

Reflect on what we have said up to this point. We are endeavouring to build a perspective that will give you a contextual feel of the progression in which you are involved. We talk of the physicality of your bodies losing their density, acquiring luminosity and beginning to glow. We talk of your Earth reaching the point when its materiality will be transformed into a pure consciousness form. We talk of your solar system, of embracing the psychological and emotional reality that you know and understand, giving you a self-sufficiency and a sense of determinism within the reality you call life. As you hurry then to achieve this point where you become consciousness, when the Earth itself becomes consciousness, when the other planets within your solar system also lose their density, you no longer have any relevance as the emotional-psychological state is redundant, for it too will transform into a different energy influence.

As this continues to evolve, as you continue to reach towards this point, you may ask the question, "Why?" Your solar system is moving through time and space, through your galaxy, but towards what? It is naturally being propelled through its own motivating forces, through its own will, to a doorway through which it will pass into anti-matter. To enable this to happen – without the total destruction of the solar system, the Earth, or you as beings – adjustments have to be made so that you can make this transition without being obliterated.

There are images within your stories for children which suggest the possibility of walking through the mirror to discover something unreal on the other side. Using this analogy, at the point of entry you will be pure consciousness, and as you pass through the doorway you will experience the polarity of what your consciousness represents and you enter into a period of negative pulsation. As you enter into the state of anti-matter itself, your functional charge becomes altered. This does not mean that you start to regress into another dense form. Quite the opposite. You are in a state of positive pulsation and your consciousness then has the ability to redistribute itself within this domain of activity.

Once you pass into the anti-matter state, you go beyond the spiritual-psychological-emotional state of being, and your state of being becomes and is what it is; you are then in a position to explore all that is. What you are at present unable to do in your current matter state is to explore all consciousness within your conscious state, as there is too much limitation, mainly through the density of your being. This does not prevent you from exploring, but it does allow you to receive explanations for things that are. What we are saying is that you will reach a time when the spiritual-psychological-emotional state or cycle will be passed through into another realm, so although the passage of matter to anti-matter and back to matter again in many ways reflects the transformation of body to spirit reverting back to body, there are fundamental differences by virtue of your evolution.

So as you pass into anti-matter you will have lost your need to be dependent on the spiritual-psychological-emotional cycle as a means of gaining understanding and you will be able to reach understanding of your own volition at will. The spiritual-psychological-emotional cycle is contained within matter even though the spiritual reality is, in your terms, beyond the material state. It still, in our terms, has a density of being. There is still personality within the spiritual state – these words are not appropriate, and we use them merely as a guide or description. There is still progression. There is no hierarchy but there are levels of enlightenment, as you have levels of enlightenment within the emotional-psychological state, so we still describe this as being within the material framework of being.

So if you regard yourselves as a complex molecule, you will have the ability to dissolve the bonds that allow the atoms to attach themselves to each other, to become disparate, either singularly or multiply, allowing your consciousness to explore the source, or sources, of its being. This allows you for the first time, in practical terms, to experience the origin of all, but only within the essence of each individual aspect as it comes from each particular point. You do not get to experience the origin from the total perspective of the group consciousness or molecule as we have described. This does not mean that you lose who you are, it merely means that you have the opportunity to explore with a greater freedom than you have previously imagined.

Passing through the Door

Is this true of the Earth as well? The organism of Earth consciousness has a different dynamic of cosmic attractability. Consequently, its need to explore and relate is contrary to your own. It naturally has the ability to draw towards it all it needs to understand. So, in this context, it still provides a focus for your life form as it will then be. It also means that you are subject to certain laws in relation to the Earth consciousness. There will still be a need for you to maintain contact with this reality, though in the context of what it will be, bears no relation to what is at present.

You carry within you the consciousness of each of the planets and moons within your solar system, and the consciousness that exists within each of these individual systems acquires a unique negative/positive equability, which allows the surface consciousness to blend with the consciousness of the planet itself, so there is a fusion. This fusion creates a greater latent force of energy than is traditionally present. This greater potential then becomes the motivating or will factor, to propel the solar system, as you know it, forwards through another door. As you pass through this door, you pass back into matter, or the reality of matter. But as you pass through, the now greater potential of those satellites within the solar system causes a unique reaction: it dematerialises altogether the physical realities as you have known them.

On passing through the door we merely have the passing

through of potential energy that contains a consciousness form. But if you were to equate your current reality with this different time-space, it would be as though there were gaps where you now have planets. However, within these gaps there is contained consciousness, and these consciousness forms, as they are no longer confined by time but more by situation, have an exactitude that is true and mathematically feasible. It is at this point that you then become as we now are.

In that time-space, we too will have passed on to further dimensions and our complexity of being will have irrevocably altered, having experienced, or been given the opportunity to experience, the source of all things as it relates to your consciousness within the anti-matter state.

It is not relevant to talk of where we were, in relation to your reality, before we passed through the anti-matter door, as we have no reference point. In practical terms, your reality did not then exist, so we have nothing to equate it with.

The reality of your consciousness, at this point, will give you a practicality that will allow you finally to communicate with, and act as ambassadors to, denser forms in your reality space as they exist, enabling you to communicate with them as we do, to teach and enlighten. This particular point of realisation has never before been reached by your race. Understand the difficulty for us, therefore, as we communicate from beyond the material. Be aware of the time, the preparation and the complexity of establishing a language that is communicable. The effort is not in the language, but in the ability to realign the energy terminals within the brain of the receiver. And a very fine – yet defined – channel needs to be created, to enable us to pass through both matter and anti-matter while maintaining contact. The structures within which you place your mind and your senses, allow you – at another level – to enjoy the contact, indeed the reality, of our existence as it is. As you receive these pulsations within the concept of your mind capacity, you allow yourselves the opportunity to experience the fullness and complexity of this being, in the out-of-time sequence of your space-time continuum – notably in your sleep. Your connection or experience of this will largely be veiled as your mind returns to the physical self. Your minds are not naturally accepting of these realities within the conscious state, therefore any effort to recollect or record the experience is likely to be perverse, misinterpreted and ultimately confusing.

When your scientists talk of the 'Big Bang' theory they have, in many ways, got it right even though fundamentally they are incorrect, as what they suggest is the annihilation of all matter, all consciousness, all being. It is true that there are those who are open to this being transformed into a totally different composition that may continue to be. What science has yet to take on board is the possibility of every living element having a life of its own, a continuum of its own, so that as you pass through any time or space warp, there is no obliteration, but merely a transposition of what already is. What science does not take into consideration is that there is a preparation for this transposition. Living matter will have evolved to a state that will enable it to make this transposition while continuing to maintain the essence of its being. This is fundamental and needs to be understood. It is impossible to merely look at the physical reality of transposition.

By their own admission there is no destruction of energy. Energy continues, energy is in perpetuity. It cannot be destroyed. This must be related, particularly to the human spiritual-psychological condition, knowing that the consciousness that is often contained within this condition does not cease to exist, that the 'bang' is not about an explosion, nor is it about a separation of all dense matter. It is not about every reality within your solar system being arbitrarily displaced somewhere else within the universe. You are a cohesive whole for a reason, and this cohesive whole will continue to evolve, transpose, transmute and re-group. Admittedly the end result, practically speaking, bears no resemblance to what you have now. But the echo, the resonance that continues through all space-time, always is and will be, so you are, you will be, always, as indeed will all that is.

We are approaching the limit of our capacity to explain your passage through time and space. Within the anti-matter state, the parallels of your experience within the matter state continue to resonate, but as there is greater movement of your consciousness form, it is possible, as far as words can allow, for you to understand the multi-dimensional nature of your being which is in the matter state in the anti-matter state. So as you return into the matter state totally transformed, your understanding of the parallel existence is total. It is at that point that you live the multi-dimensional nature of your being, all at the same time. It is not that you are travellers, it is merely that you can spread your con-sciousness form over a wide set of co-ordinates that embrace time. You are, therefore, the wave motion. All energy has a particular motion, no matter how infinitesimal. There is a wave motion, there is continuum, even beyond the resulting matter state, into other realities. It is not practical to explain.

When you reach the state where we are now, you will attain flexibility of, let us say, movement. You will contain within you what has been gained practically through experience, which will allow you to relate to the denser realities that need assistance in interpreting their own understanding. You will facilitate conditions of operations –

it is easiest for us to say karmic laws – and you will guide these other realities through the pathways of understanding so that they are able to receive and reflect on their own progression. You then become 'enablers'. You will also be actively aware of your own future. You will, in simple terms, be more conscious of what needs to be accomplished. There is very little, in your terms, that will be wasted as a result. You will become more effective. Your memory will become more expansive, more complete. As a result of this complete memory, at any point that you receive 'distress-resonance' from other realities, you may then approach and facilitate understanding where possible. You become universal trouble-shooters. The terms are not accurate, but they will suffice for the moment. Having experienced for yourselves the potential imbalance of the need to struggle, to ask and receive assistance from others, means you will have the memory of the practical experience within your memory data-base and will be more alert to the practical needs of the denser realities. You will operate in closer conjunction with the one law. The law of truth, the law of love, the law of consistency which permeates the universal framework, and you will work in closer contact with its meaning in the essence of its being.

Having given a broader picture of your extending reality through time, allow yourselves now to contemplate the enormous changes that need to be made within your reality at the present moment and over the coming decades. There is much to be done, much to be achieved, to be learnt and understood. It is time for you to take on board the possibility of your own ability to communicate. This does not have to be in the guise in which this communicator works. It is natural and innate in every one of you, and all of you have the capacity to communicate in this way if you can trust yourselves sufficiently to allow yourselves to accept the reality, the hidden reality in which you live that is not part of the illusion.

Communication, as it has evolved, must be looked at metaphorically. You have been led and guided in forms of communication that allow you to become aware of the other realities embracing your own. The metaphors continue. The illusion is a metaphor. All structures are metaphoric. If you step from behind your mask you will see. Take the courage to remove the mask. Do not just peep but face, fully and objectively, your reality. None of you need to be deceived if you so choose. It is not always necessary for you to know. You work on the basis of organising beliefs so that they provide you with a reality within which you can operate. It is enough to become aware of your intuition, your feelings, your sensory perceptions, which you all have. Allow those to steer you, to signpost your way towards greater under-standing and a more dynamic focus on your individual and group progression.

Allow your hearts to dictate your needs more. The intuitive feelings that you receive are broadly and soundly based on what is appropriate. The mind allows you to exercise subjective consciousness. This subjective conscious-ness is the vehicle, the projectile that can bring you to under-standing, but in itself is not the receptacle of the under-standing – that is the consciousness you have contained within. So using the projectile as a force, or device, to seek, hold and retrieve consciousness or understanding, and bringing it back down into your receptacle, is the best way in which it can be employed. In itself, it has limited function. Its function is vital as it allows you to question, but the answers are floating around you: aim your arrow wherever you feel is most appropriate and draw back towards you that which you need to understand, and allow it to germinate within. There is no struggle here! You experience impatience, restlessness and despair if you feel you are not receiving the answers. We merely say that you are not listening in the correct manner. Do not misinterpret that which is conscious as being consciousness. Being conscious of consciousness is merely focusing on the projectile, not on the receptacle that can receive and foster understanding.

We have no motivating influence for communicating this information. You have. We are available to facilitate, within limiting factors, information that we anticipate may be productive to those of you who can listen with receptive ears. By virtue of your being, you emit a harmonic from the surface of your planet. In many ways it is a distress signal from your consciousness, within the context we have described. In adverse circumstances this distress signal alerts the memory of our own adverse experience. In your terms, a need is then evoked within the vibration, as we understand it, of love. This facilitates a co-operation, and the need for us to co-operate with the origin of the distress signal. We then endeavour to isolate those through whom we can communicate.

It is necessary for us to become compatible with those who in your reality desire to communicate, as this desire stems from their own spiritual contract to achieve and to serve. In many ways, there is a mutual sense of devotion to duty, to which we are both responding. Collectively, therefore, we isolate an individual or group through whom we can communicate. We then take on a particular – we do not have the correct word – but let us say 'organic' composition, to transfer specific aspects of knowledge that we feel are needed within the laws that we both operate.

Consequently, once our communication is finished, the organic composition from sun-consciousness will disperse, or rather, it is unlikely that we will regroup in the same way. Two factors are involved: firstly, the harmonic of every individual has a particular frequency so we need to adapt; secondly, it is necessary for us to take into consideration the evolution of the individual through whom we are contacting you. As we have explained, there is a multi-dimensional mechanic of operation here. In many ways we are activating the consciousness that is contained within this communicator, so he is, in many respects, speaking from his own experience out-of-time. It is not easy to make you aware of the complexity of communication. Until this point you have used communication in very simple terms, within very simple definitions. The time has come, through your own achievement, to now be able to expand the metaphor, to allow you to enjoy a more complex explanation of how things are and how communication is facilitated.

Focus once more on the image in the centre of your circle, and observe the spiral at the apex of the pyramid. Sense yourself descending into the pyramid to mingle with the multi-coloured flowers, gradually letting the spiral of energy dissolve. Allow the pyramidal structure to ascend out of view. Feel your senses returning, and watch the vision of the flowers disappear. In the context of this communion, we suspend the discourse. Until the next time.

TEN

The Timeless Whole

Focus on the centre of a circle. Visualise a vortex of energy descending from the floor downwards. See it like a whirlpool of water so that it is imbued with the essence of the spirit. The momentum is downwards – not that you are drawn into it, but it brings down from above that which needs to descend to make its presence known within the framework and space in which we work.

Imagine yourself sitting at the edge, suspended at the edge of the vortex. Allow yourself to feel the cool, ionised air that should be present; it should enervate, stimulate and calm the mind-body. Absorb the healing and harmonising qualities that reflect from it.

It is perhaps most appropriate to speak now of wholeness of being. We have taken certain aspects of your development, of your progress, through time. We have created a picture that may illuminate the assembly of interconnecting formations within which you are placed and united. We may have given you an appreciation of a greater whole, of a larger

context within which you communicate. Do understand that these words have been given to activate your mind into discovering, within your own consciousness sources, that which is viable and truthful for you. Communication is given not as de facto knowledge, but merely as a taster for what is really present. To allow you to make your own discoveries and to enable you to enquire sufficiently about your own uniqueness of being, about that which is for you.

You are walking organisms of truth. This is what you believe in, so this is what you are. This is what you see, so this is what you are. If you wish to change what you are, you need to change what you believe. To change what you believe, you only have to change one impulse of that wealth of belief structure to actually dismantle the entire structure and then rebuild it around the belief you have changed. Consequently you become someone else. If you wish to be someone else, you change what you believe. If you wish to see something different from what you are, you have to create an image of what you wish to see before it becomes real. To understand what you need to know, you must facilitate the placing of understanding within your being before this can be evoked into conscious knowledge.

To be conscious of consciousness is not sufficient. This is merely a superficial application, which means that you pass over the substantial content of consciousness itself. To know is to be. So we ask the question: "How do you be?" Is it possible just to be? More importantly, can you accept yourself as merely being, or is it necessary for you to continually prove to yourself that you be and continue to be. As a result, you continually re-state who you are by virtue of what you be. But this momentum becomes cyclical, and you get caught in a cycle of events that perpetuate themselves within the context of familiarity.

So perhaps you need to step outside your being. Perhaps you need to embrace something else apart from that which you believe you have within yourself. Whether this is a new feeling, a new concept, a new belief. But as you embrace other potential impulses from outside, as this frees you from the cycle of familiarity, you embrace the freedom and explore the new space that are offered as a result. You do not pass merely into another cycle of belief which, again, will perpetuate itself within its own comfortableness of being.

This age is a time of responsibility. Allow yourself to accept this responsibility and to take the freedom that is being offered, to peruse through the all-embracing totality of consciousness in all its forms as it pervades all things. Allow your mind to leave the familiarity and comfortableness of your thinking mode and project your mind into different areas of consciousness. Bring back those impulses into yourself, allowing them to evoke within you your own understanding. Let them relate to you so that they become personal, meaningful and loving. You are naturally what you create, but if there is no limit to what you can create, the potential is also limitless.

The effort and difficulty are in accepting the multi-dimensional nature of your being, of the various ways in which you can be creative. Who are you to have such talents? Who are you to focus these talents into singular expressions of creativity? You are who you are. You are all connected to your own unique points of origin. You have the ability to build the bridges between where you are now and your origin. Those secrets of your origin are locked within you, within the consciousness that you bring from without into the dense matter of your body. It is all there.

Much will reveal itself of its own accord as you work with yourself, as you accept your personal power. Accepting it and expressing it is the most difficult thing for you to do, but express it you must. It is an active momentum, not a passive one. Open your arms. Do not expect someone to come towards you; walk in and surrender to it. Surrender is closer to acceptance than denial of Self, for what you are accepting is your own uniqueness of being, not someone else's, and not an idea or concept, but the very nature of your being. Within this being-ness there is total communication, giving you complete access to everything that is in abundance in the universe.

The Silence within Words

We hear you say, "but", we hear you say, "we have limit-ations", "we cannot see". Accept your limitations. Maybe these limitations will then become strengths, ladders which you can scale, and as you reach the top you can see what was previously not visible. Are you worthy? What are you going to do with the words that you have read in this book. Does it matter? Do you have to do anything at all? Or is it sufficient to join with others at a particular level and merely absorb the essence behind these words?

Each and every one of you knows what you need to do. You have an appreciation of the heights you need to reach towards to be able to satisfy your needs. To be aware is the greatest gift of all. This means that you are in an accepting mode, that you are in surrender, with your arms open, prepared to receive. Is this enough then, to be alert and aware? Isn't there more we could be doing?

Listen to the words as you say them in your mind. As you finish saying the word alert the word is suddenly cut off and there is a suspension of energy left hanging. Listen again. There is a silence. And what is written in the silence? There is a universe of understanding, and this understanding is reflective of the moment. Listen to the word aware. The word actually does not finish, it is drawn out over a period of indefinite time. It is like a radar screen, with the beam of light circling around it. It is continuous. Listen to it again. It is looking, probing, seeking. Allow yourselves to enjoy the dynamic of words. They are complex mathematical configurations of sound and tonality which of themselves are imbued with certain textural qualities and colour. As we link words together to form sentences we can also look at what is between the words, between the sentences, and this is equally powerful. Indeed often it is more powerful than the words themselves.

There are those who teach in silence, who bring down an energy, a consciousness form that will naturally work with you, depending on your need, at any specific time. Your greatest endeavour is not to give the unknown values of tangibility, as this merely restricts that which is known and available for all to be known. Sometimes it is sufficient to keep this understanding at this level, until you allow the knowingness to permeate your being, merely as an energy force itself, allowing it to nudge, release, or keep hidden, what is appropriate at any given time.

You occupy co-ordinates of what you might call five-dimensional time-space. As you picture this in your mind, extend it so that you have realities dovetailing with other realities, encapsulated within more distant realities which extend you beyond your own time-space co-ordinates. There are other dimensions beyond the fifth, taking you into parallel dimensions and beyond matter; these are beyond the current definition of your scientific endeavours. Allow them to be there and to work with you. You may understand in the instant what they are about, but as you start to apply this to rational thought, it may escape you. If so, leave the experience at the level where you encountered it and understand that from that experience perhaps something will be evoked that is fresh and new in your terms. We are speaking of communication, of a form of total communication that goes beyond the notion of spirituality, of cosmology, beyond all the 'ologies' and 'isms'. You have given yourselves time to prove that there is more than life.

Science understands and knows more than is made known within your reality. Governments know more than they reveal. If all these unknowns and uncommunicables were placed together honestly, with free access given to everyone, even more would be known. You yourselves would relax more into accepting the inexplicable, and be relaxed about it.

Accepting the Unknown

You strive so, you work hard. This is acknowledged. But why put effort into something that does not require it? Why is something only working when you put effort into making it so? In your most inspirational moments nothing occurs, because you are in a state of total balance of knowing; you are able to access what this represents and communicate it. Everything else outside of this inspirational level of operation involves too much work. The desire for you to know what is coming your way has a counter-momentum to you being unaware of what is coming and accepting what happens at the time of occurrence. If you do not know what is coming, you are far more open and flexible and you deal with what comes in a more effective way. If you have an awareness of what is coming, you immediately start evaluating it before it arrives, assessing if it is what you were made aware of. A lot of time and energy goes into validating whether this is accurate, so much so that often the experience is gone and you have not had time to either enjoy it or relate to it at the level that you needed to. Do you need to be so dependent and selfish to know what is coming your way, knowing therefore that this might intrude on what the experience has to offer to you in the first instance? Do you continually need to validate the experience? Have you so little trust of yourselves that you cannot just accept what you experience? Are you so dependent on outside circumstances to confirm for you that which you already have the ability to know and assess for yourselves?

This is why we say the reality of your sensitives and psychics is changing. The dynamic now is different. You need to be responsible and to accept the power of this responsibility. Psychics will work with you in a different way. They will start to project the realities with which they are involved. They will be able to magnetise intelligent forms from other realities within the proximity of their energetic being, allowing them to communicate directly with you. This will be your future proof. But understand that you will only have this proof when you can accept what it has to offer.

These words, we are aware, may seem abstract and a little elusive, but you will have the opportunity to confirm them for yourselves. You are reaching a time of total communication, when you can accept all realities as one, as indeed they are. There is no separation. The words and descriptions we use are illustrative. The great pioneers of spiritual communication have established a reality of the spirit. There are now people creating awarenessess beyond that.

Are you prepared to accept the reality of change? Each of you, check whether you have asked yourselves this question before. If you have not, then are you prepared to accept the reality of change? Are you prepared to accept the reality that is presented as a result of this change, and will you own it and live it as your own? If the answers to these questions are yes, you have nothing to fear. There will be no anxiety but merely trust. If the answers are no, you will have difficulty because you are not in a state of trust with yourselves, and you have a need to avoid experience because of the, perhaps, unpleasant things that might be contained within it, or perhaps because of the change that you need to embrace as a result of having this experience. Then you have to ask the fundamental question: "Why am I afraid of experience?" These questions are not only asked of you here, they are also asked of those who are not; and as communicators, these are questions that you can ask of others.

The mind is a vehicle. It is always in continuous motion. The body is a receptacle. If there is anything that the body needs, the mind potentially has the power to go out and identify it, and return it to the receptacle. As your mind is alerted by your consciousness to what you need, it leaves, identifies and retrieves this need, which is then brought back to feed the consciousness and the consciousness can then reveal that which it already knows. In many ways this is closely allied to what you call clairvoyance, but in the context of understanding and progressive movement through time, it has greater meaning.

Your flora and fauna communicate in exactly the same way, with the exception that they are totally instinctive as they do not work on the basis of the left and right brain principle. Their consciousnesses have different energetic formations and their ability to be immediately more responsive to any situation has greater potential, but the principle of consciousness is the same. The principle of having a source is the same – an energetic source, a conceptual point of being as a source. And you all respond ultimately to the same impulse.

Outside the parameters of word structure, there are other beings present as we speak these words, who have been drawn close to observe. Such is the energetic radiance within the building where these words were spoken that it is now acting as a transmitter in its own right, to draw towards it new intelligence, different forms of enlightening capabilities, who can work with those who come within the parameters of this building.

You can create other similar structures in other places, which will allow other consciousnesses to draw close. As you form other points of contact and meeting, you will create, if you like, magnetic poles that will hold a greater energy, and this greater energy can attract towards it the activation of different intelligences.

The intelligent forms that they embrace include those who have experience within the spiritual-emotional cycle. They observe the tonality of your spiritual beings, giving themselves a better opportunity to understand evolving communication as it relates to you, and ways that this can be better facilitated by them. Having been given this opportunity for them to draw close, the structure that has been created through the communicating of this book will be ever present, allowing them the opportunity to draw near. The energetic vibration on which you now mentally stand suspended, allows them to come close. These are not guides or helpers as you have traditionally defined them, but individual sources of intelligence who can co-operate with the evocation of your own consciousness, allowing the guidance they give to be more direct and tangible.

Shortly after the turn of the millennium, some of these beings will be able to make themselves manifest within the energetic environment of certain people who are reading these words. So close are you now to this radical change in communication, as it has been defined, and what is currently being presented to you is your own understanding of Self. The group work, which is being put into practice at a group level around your Earth, is to bring people to accept an understanding of who they are. This is the momentum. This is the dynamic. This is what is important.

You can tap into our key note of resonance by tuning into your alerted state, then listen! Whatever you hear within your mind is that which it is. You cannot hear anything else. Meditation, as you know it, does not facilitate movement to the alerted state. There is difficulty with the word meditation as each individual has a different concept and application of what this means to them, which is why we say meditation does not help. We use the term projecting the mind, knowing that your mind is not confined by time or space, and that you can place it within whatever reality you wish; merely thinking it there is sufficient. But if you place yourself within an unfamiliar reality of which you have no experience, you then have to ask yourself, "How can I trust what I am given?" So you must allow yourself to become familiar with your need before you place yourself within these situations.

If you use meditation as a way to elevate the vibration of your mind, allowing you to project your mind outside your realm of normal activity, then yes, meditation is useful. If you use meditation as a passive exploration of the astral planes surrounding you, then no, it is not. There is a huge percentage of the mind yet unexplored. You have the capability of exploring that by releasing your mind from the environment of your experience, and allowing it to embrace other realities of which you may not be conscious. But vibrationally, as you bring your mind back to yourself, you also bring back the experience each time that you do this; even though it may seem you have not succeeded, we say this is impossible. The more you apply yourself in this way, the more experience you bring back to yourself. And, if the impulse comes from the consciousness source itself, what it brings back is that which it needs to receive. Consequently those hidden parts, those secret matters, can then slowly be revealed.

As we have explained, consciousness comes from a free point within the universe. This is the source of your being which you bring into your physical reality. There are many terms which are often restricted that we call the soul, the spirit, the source of wisdom. You may call it understanding without knowledge. What is the higher self? The higher self, in many ways, is the higher mind, the vibration of the mind that is beyond the material. You have free access to your spiritual source as you are part of the spiritual cycle and emotional condition we describe. You have the potential to move outside of this reality, but you can only do it by freeing your mind.

Do remember that your mind, once it leaves the parameters of your existence, is not embodied within the emotional context. It is free to move through space, to experience whatever realities are there. If you are talking about the astral journey, experiencing your own spiritual source, this is quite different. You must be very specific within your own mind now of what journey you are talking about. We do stress the difference. To confuse matters, all words and descriptions are metaphoric. It is difficult to encapsulate something that is beyond the material, and the words and descriptions that we use are pictorial to allow you to activate the unstimulated known areas of the brain-mind context, which are not consciously employed on a day-to-day basis.

What we are talking about is something outside the psycho-spiritual context. Within meditation as it has been traditionally taught, you have the ability to move through the astral body, to experience the spiritual reality. If you move outside the spiritual reality into the physical confines of the universe itself, there is the need to project the mind. That is all.

Communication as you have previously experienced it will become diminished as it acquires its own context, its own degree of perfection. Some are still currently caught up in their own realities within the astral context – be they restrictive or unrestrictive. As these become resolved, as those who are able to pass from the physical into the spiritual context are able to help release those who are still in the lower vibrational states of the astral plane, and as those who are within the physical context allow themselves to explore the astral context while still being in the physical state, there will be greater freedom of movement.

As the present influence from the lower astral state on to your psychological-emotional being is cleared, there will be less lower vibrational influence, in the simplest terms possible, around you on a day-to-day basis. This will mean that, in crude terms, you are less susceptible to moods and to feelings that are not your own. You currently react, totally unconsciously, to clouds of energy, clouds of emotions, which are influenced from the astral realm and come into your reality. As the astral plane itself becomes more purified, the need for you to experience that reality will diminish as you then allow yourself to know that experience within you. Again, it is difficult for us to describe as we have no experience of the emotional context, and the translation and interpretation of what we are conveying are being transposed by another energy.

The purification, as we see it, of this level or plane of existence, will largely coincide with your period of de-materialisation into consciousness itself. It is a coming together of all forces as one, in the one time. Those of you who engage in spiritual development and awareness, are actually clearing your resonant contact with the astral level. Your increase in sensitivity means that you no longer carry within your psychological-emotional make-up the protective experience which is progressive. It is simpler to say that it is like totally peeling away a layer from your being, and that you will have to learn to develop another way to desensitise yourself from this increasing sensitivity. But with this increase in sensitivity comes a greater sense of knowing, and it is this knowing that comes from your consciousness – or from your soul if you prefer – that allows you to deal practically with the situation. It is difficult for us to clinically state the process as we merely observe what is happening.

As we say these words, you may be wondering how it is possible to desensitise yourself, or protect yourself, from the electro-magnetic energies that seem to be increasing from videos and televisions, and from emanations of negativity from hoards of people who seem to be absorbing it rapidly.

Quite simply, it is not possible. However, there are two basic principles here that, as your awareness of these influences increases, you can practically learn to pace yourself in relation to their existence. First, you cannot escape the reality of their presence. Secondly, the strength of your knowing creates a principle inside yourself which first of all alerts you to this fact, and then stops you empathising with the situation. As you allow yourself to be more objective, and if you see this reality, you then have this objectivity. As you see this reality you have, in simple terms, the ability to deflect it. This means that, in the situation itself, you are still subject to this reality, but are not part of it, although you get a sense of its effect. It is only once you are outside of this reality that you can revert to your normal, vibrant, self.

Within the context of this communication, we will now disengage ourselves and disperse to the origin of our reality. The combination, cohesion, of our being, once dispersed, will not have the same configuration in other circumstances. Each situation has a different magnetic attractability and our coming together again, as it will happen, will take on other contextual manifestations. Your communicator talks of working with the mind, of activating intelligence, of allowing you to think, feel and sense for yourself. It is because of what he embodies that we have been attracted to what he represents. It is not always productive to have such a public outlet as we have been privileged to experience.

Most of what we speak of is taught silently. It is not time to give such pre-eminence to what can be said within the context of this framework of communication. Most of you are developing a contact outside of your spiritual-psychological-emotional context. This is largely unconscious, but some of you already know that you have an ability to sense that this is happening, or has happened. Be confident of what you sense. Nobody can teach you of its appropriateness, validity, or correctness, only you have the ability to know. It is difficult, therefore, to speak publicly about that which you understand, but do know that this group is reflected elsewhere many, many times.

There is now a gathering of like minds in a way that has not been previously possible, where re-definition and looking for the new, have a momentum beyond your realisation. There are those who are afraid, or who are cautious, to speak out. There is still some sense of unacceptability within those who have highly structured beliefs. In these instances be private, but trust your knowing. You should not need validation of what you know outside of yourself. As well as challenging, this time also reflects difficulty, and provokes restlessness within you as you are embracing an awareness of what is coming your way without being able to voice exactly what it is. We respect the restlessness.

Part of our presence here is to give, where possible, some reassurance within limited forms of communication of what is happening, of how you are communicating, how you are connected, and where you are progressing to. We appreciate that these can merely be concepts, ideas perhaps, things which are largely intangible. We understand the struggle, the difficulties and often the disbelief. Continue to look, to be alert and aware. That is all.

The context of who we are will resonate for some time to come. The mental structures that you have created, the energetic structures that have been facilitated through this communication, will be ever-present for some time. Know this, and in the privacy of your own home, connect with the energy structures that have been created. It is already in your mind, but to give it added emphasis, you can mentally place yourself in these energy structures and activate that which is already within you. This will allow you to recreate within yourself everything that you have experienced within these words.

As we leave, we place above your head a 42-pointed star. Know that this is there. In your own private time with yourself, try to visualise this in your mind. Place yourself within it and use it as a vehicle of transportation, and allow it to show you its secrets. It contains within it the properties of gold, silver, platinum and strontium, representing the preciousness of your planet, and a more reactive element, giving the star an instability, and the potential to transform and to leap into different areas of consciousness.

Focus now on the whirlpool of water, and see yourself floating above it. Allow the stem of the whirlpool to come up to the surface, so that you are now suspended above a lake, calm, clear, reflective of your own spiritual nature. Take a moment, as it becomes a mirror. Look in the mirror to see reflected that which is above.

As we disengage we give you our love, we offer our guidance and co-operation in truth and in harmony towards a greater end, in time, through time, in perpetuity.